John Henry Newman

Sermons preached on various occasions

John Henry Newman

Sermons preached on various occasions

ISBN/EAN: 9783741175664

Manufactured in Europe, USA, Canada, Australia, Japa

Cover: Foto ©Andreas Hilbeck / pixelio.de

John Henry Newman

Sermons preached on various occasions

SERMONS

PREACHED

ON VARIOUS OCCASIONS.

BY

JOHN HENRY NEWMAN, D.D.,

OF THE ORATORY.

SECOND EDITION.

LONDON:
BURNS AND LAMBERT.
MDCCCLVIII.

[The right of translation is reserved.]

TO THE VERY REVEREND

HENRY EDWARD MANNING, D.D.,

PROVOST OF WESTMINSTER,

ETC., ETC.

My Dear Dr. Manning,

On this day, when you are celebrating the opening of your new Church and Mission at Bayswater, I am led to hope, since I cannot give you my presence on so happy an occasion, that you will accept from me this small Volume instead, as my act of devotion to the great St. Charles, St. Philip's friend, and your Patron, and as some sort of memorial of the friendship which there has been between us for nearly thirty years.

I am, my dear Dr. Manning,
Ever yours affectionately,
JOHN H. NEWMAN,
of the Oratory.

In Fest. Visitat. B.M.V.
1857.

ADVERTISEMENT.

When the Author was preparing for the serious step, which he took nearly twelve years ago, of embracing the Catholic Religion, it was, if not his intention, at least his expectation, that he should never write again on any doctrinal subject. He was able to fancy himself, in the time then before him, discussing questions of philosophy or ecclesiastical history; nor did he exclude religious controversy, criticism, or literature, from his view; but it seemed to him incongruous that one, who had so freely taught and published error in a Protestant communion, should put himself forward as a dogmatic teacher in the Catholic Church.

This disinclination to engage in the more sacred departments of Theology was increased, first, by his finding his vocation already fixed, before he had had the opportunity of going through the regular scholastic course; and next, by the circumstance, that the Congregation, in which that vocation lay, had ever placed its formal duties in practical work, and had not commonly directed even the personal talents or private labours or leisure hours of its members towards the discussion or illustration of Catholic doctrine.

On the other hand, the ordinary duties of a missionary priest have necessarily exacted of him to some extent, and have accordingly justified, the assumption of a teacher's office; and the unexpected honour of a Degree in Theology, conferred on him from Rome, without the ordinary exercises, would have been no slight encouragement to him to undertake that office, had he been otherwise minded to do so.

However, he has been faithful on the whole to the rule or anticipation, which he set before him on becoming a Catholic. Why he has departed from it in the present and one other instance, it is not worth while to explain. He will but observe, that his Volume of "Discourses to Mixed Congregations", implies by its title, that it is polemical and hortatory after all, rather than dogmatic, and addressed to those who are external to the Church. This is partly the case also with the Sermons contained in the present Volume; not to say that its title too, announcing that they have been elicited by particular occasions, carries with it the apology, that they are the result of external circumstances rather than of any set purpose of his own.

He takes the opportunity of its directly religious character to ask of all those who feel an interest in his past or present, to suffer it to be a call on them to bear in mind in their charitable prayers his future and his end. He has no intention that this should be the last of his Volumes; but the last must come sooner or later, and the catalogue must be completed and sealed up; nor, at the age to which he has already attained, should he ever have reason to be surprised, if he were not allowed the time or the power to add to their number.

He has only to observe, as regards the Sermons which this Volume contains, that the first eight, the tenth, and the eleventh, were preached in High Mass, and written before delivery; the ninth and the twelfth have been composed from the original notes, the former of them immediately after delivery, the latter at this date. It must be added that two of them, the ninth and tenth, have been already published, and a third, the eleventh, has been already in print.

And he must further observe, that in consequence of his using different editions of the Douay Version of Scripture according to the occasion, the translated text, as his Volume presents it, will not be found in any one copy of that Version which a reader may be in the habit of using.

July 2, 1857.

CONTENTS.

ight Sermons preached before the Catholic University of Ireland in 1856–1857, being the first year of the opening of its Church.

1. Intellect, the instrument of Religious Training,
   St. Monica. p. 1.

2. The Religion of the Pharisee, the religion of Mankind,
   10th Pentecost. p. 20.

3. Waiting for Christ, . . 27th Pentecost. p. 41.

4. The Secret Power of Divine Grace,
   28th Pentecost. p. 62.

5. Dispositions for Faith, . . 4th Advent. p. 79.

6. Omnipotence in Bonds, . . Epiphany. p 100.

7. St. Paul's Characteristic Gift,
   Conversion of St. Paul. p. 121.

8. St. Paul's Gift of Sympathy, . Sexagesima. p. 141.

'reached in St. Chad's, Birmingham, on occasion of the Installation of the first Bishop of the See.

9. Christ upon the Waters, . October, 27th, 1850. p. 162.

Preached at Oscott, in the first Provincial Synod of Westminster.

10. The Second Spring, . July 13th, 1852. p. 2

Preached in the first Diocesan Synod of Birmingham.

11. Order, the Witness and Instrument of Unity.

November 9th, 1853. p. 2

Preached in the Oratory, Birmingham, on occasion of its first anniversary.

12. The Mission of St. Philip Neri,

January 15th and 18th, 1850. p. 2

SERMON I.

INTELLECT, THE INSTRUMENT OF RELIGIOUS TRAINING.

Evang. Sec. Luc., c. vii. v. 12.

Cum autem appropinquaret portæ civitatis, ecce defunctus efferebatur filius unicus matris suæ: et hæc vidua erat.

And when He came nigh to the gate of the city, behold, a dead man was carried out, the only son of his mother: and she was a widow.

THIS day we celebrate one of the most remarkable feasts in the Calendar. We commemorate a saint who gained the heavenly crown by prayers indeed and tears, by sleepless nights and weary wanderings, but not in the administration of any high office in the Church, not in the fulfilment of some great resolution or special counsel; not as a preacher, teacher, evangelist, reformer, or champion of the faith; not as Bishop of the flock, or temporal governor; not by eloquence, by wisdom, or by controversial success; not in the way of any other saint whom we invoke in the circle of the year; but as a mother, seeking and gaining by her penances the conversion of her son. It was for no ordinary son that she prayed, and it was no ordinary supplication by which she gained him. When a holy man saw its vehemence, ere it was successful, he said to her, "Go in peace; the son of such prayers cannot perish". The prediction was fulfilled beyond its letter; not only was that young man converted, but after his conversion he became a saint; not only a saint but a doctor also, and "instructed many unto justice". St. Augustine was the son for whom she prayed; and if he has been a luminary for all ages of the Church since, many thanks do we owe to his mother, St. Monica, who, having borne him in the flesh, travailed for him in the spirit.

The Church, in her choice of a gospel for this feast, has likened St. Monica to the desolate widow whom our Lord met at the gate of the city, as she was going forth to bury the corpse of her only son. He saw her, and said, "Weep not"; and He touched the bier, and the dead arose. St. Monica asked and obtained a more noble miracle. Many a mother who is anxious for her son's bodily welfare, neglects his soul. So did not the Saint of to-day; her son might be

accomplished, eloquent, able, and distinguished;
all this was nothing to her while he was dead
in God's sight, while he was the slave of sin,
while he was the prey of heresy. She desired
his true life. She wearied heaven with prayer,
and wore out herself with praying; she did
not at once prevail. He left his home; he
was carried forward by his four bearers, ignorance, pride, appetite, and ambition; he was carried out into a foreign land, he crossed over from
Africa to Italy. She followed him, she followed
the corpse, the chief, the only mourner; she went
where he went, from city to city. It was nothing
to her to leave her dear home and her native soil;
she had no country below; her sole rest, her sole
repose, her *Nunc dimittis*, was his new birth.
So while she still walked forth in her deep anguish and isolation, and her silent prayer, she
was at length rewarded by the long-coveted miracle. Grace melted the proud heart, and purified the corrupt breast of Augustine, and restored
and comforted his mother; and hence, in to-day's
Collect, the Almighty Giver is especially addressed as "Mœrentium consolator et in Te
sperantium salus"; the consoler of those that
mourn, and the health of those who hope.

And thus Monica, as the widow in the gospel, becomes an image of Holy Church, who is ever lamenting over her lost children, and by her importunate prayers, ever recovering them from the grave of sin; and to Monica, as the Church's representative, may be addressed those words of the Prophet: "Put off, O Jerusalem, the garments of thy mourning and affliction; arise, and look about towards the East, and behold thy children; for they went out from thee on foot, led by the enemies; but the Lord will bring them to thee exalted with honour, as children of the kingdom".

This, I say, is not a history of past time merely, but of every age. Generation passes after generation, and there is on the one side the same doleful, dreary wandering, the same feverish unrest, the same fleeting enjoyments, the same abiding and hopeless misery; and on the other, the same anxiously beating heart of impotent affection. Age goes after age, and still Augustine rushes forth again and again, with his young ambition, and his intellectual energy, and his turbulent appetites; educated, yet untaught; with powers strengthened, sharpened, refined by exercise, but unenlightened and untrained,—goes forth into the world, ardent, self-willed, reckless, headstrong, inexperienced, to fall into the hands of those who seek his life, and to become the victim of heresy and sin. And still, again and again does hapless Monica weep; weeping for that dear child who grew up with her from the womb, and of whom she is now robbed; of whom she has lost sight; wandering with him in his wanderings, following his steps in her imagination, cherishing his image in her heart, keeping his name upon her lips, and feeling withal, that, as a woman, she is unable to cope with the violence and the artifices of the world. And still again and again does Holy Church take her part and her place, with a heart as tender and more strong, with an arm, and an eye, and an intellect more powerful than hers, with an influence more than human, more sagacious than the world, and more religious than home, to restrain and reclaim those whom passion, or example, or sophistry is hurrying forward to destruction.

My Brethren, there is something happy in the circumstance, that the first Sunday of our academical worship should fall on the feast of St. Monica. For is not this one chief aspect of a University, and an aspect which it especially bears in this sacred place, to supply that which that memorable Saint so much desiderated, and for which she attempted to compensate by her prayers? Is it not one part of our especial office to receive those from the hands of father and mother, whom father and mother can keep no longer? Thus, while professing all sciences, and speaking by the mouths of philosophers and sages, a University delights in the well-known appellation of " Alma Mater". She is a mother who, after the pattern of that greatest and most heavenly of mothers, is, on the one hand, " Mater Amabilis", and " Causa nostræ lætitiæ", and on the other, " Sedes Sapientiæ" also. She is a mother, living, not in the seclusion of the family, and in the garden's shade, but in the wide world, in the populous and busy town, claiming, like our great Mother, the meek and tender Mary, " to praise her own self, and to glory, and to open her mouth", because she alone has, " compassed the circuit of Heaven, and penetrated into the bottom of the deep, and walked upon the waves of the sea", and in every department of human learning, is able to confute and put right those who would set knowledge against itself, and would make truth contradict truth, and would persuade the world that, to be religious, you must be ignorant, and to be intellectual, you must be unbelieving.

My meaning will be clearer, if I revert to the nature and condition of the human mind. The human mind, as you know, my Brethren, may be regarded from two principal points of view, as intellectual and as moral. As intellectual, it apprehends truth; as moral, it apprehends duty. The perfection of the intellect is called ability and talent; the perfection of our moral nature is virtue. And it is our great misfortune here, and our trial, that, as things are found in the world, the two are separated, and independent of each other; that, where power of intellect is, there need not be virtue; and that where right, and goodness, and moral greatness are, there need not be talent. It was not so in the beginning; not that our nature is essentially different from what it was when first created; but that the Creator, upon its creation, raised it above itself by a supernatural grace, which blended together all its faculties, and made them conspire into one whole, and act in common towards one end; so that, had the race continued in that blessed state of privilege, there never would have been distance, rivalry, hostility between one faculty and another. It is otherwise now; so much the worse for us;—the grace is gone; the soul cannot hold together; it falls to pieces; its elements strive with each other. And as, when a kingdom has long been in a state of tumult, sedition, or rebellion, certain portions break off from the whole and from the central government, and set up for themselves; so is it with the soul of man. So is it, I say, with the soul, long ago,—that a number of small kingdoms, independent of each other and at war with each other, have arisen in it, such and so many as to reduce the original sovereignty to a circuit of territory and to an influence not more considerable than they have themselves. And all these small dominions, as I may call them, in the soul, are, of course, one by one, incomplete and defective, strong in some points, weak in others, because not any one of them is the whole, sufficient for itself, but only one part of the whole, which, on the contrary, is made up of all the faculties of the soul together. Hence you find in one man, or one set of men, the reign, as I may call it, the acknowledged reign of passion or appetite; among others, the avowed reign of brute strength and material resources; among others, the reign of intellect; and among others (and would they were many!) the more excellent reign of virtue. Such is the state of things, as it shows to us, when we cast our eyes abroad into the world; and every one, when he comes to years of discretion, and begins to think, has all these separate powers warring in his own breast,—appetite, passion, secular ambition, intellect, and conscience, and trying severally to get possession of him. And, when he looks out of himself, he sees them all severally embodied on a grand scale, in large establishments and centres, outside of him, one here, and another there, in aid of that importunate canvass, so to express myself, which each of them is carrying on within him. And thus, at least for a time, he is in a state of internal strife, confusion, and uncertainty, first attracted this way, then that, not knowing how to choose, though sooner or later choose he must; or rather, he must choose soon, and cannot choose late, for he cannot help thinking, speaking, and acting; and to think, speak, and act, is to choose.

This is a very serious state of things; and what makes it worse is, that these various faculties and powers of the human mind have so long been separated from each other, so long cultivated and developed each by itself, that it comes to be taken for granted that they cannot be united; and it is commonly thought, because some men follow duty, others pleasure, others glory, and others intellect, therefore that one of these things excludes the other; that duty cannot be pleasant, that virtue cannot be intellectual, that goodness cannot be great, that conscientiousness cannot be heroic; and the fact is often so, I grant, that there *is* a separation, though I deny its necessity. I grant, that, from the disorder and confusion into which the human mind has fallen, too often good men are not attractive, and bad men are; too often cleverness, or wit, or taste, or richness of fancy, or keenness of intellect, or depth, or knowledge, or pleasantness and agreeableness, is on the side of error and not on the side of virtue. Excellence, as things are, does lie, I grant, in more directions than one, and it is ever easier to excel in one thing than in two. If then a man has more talent, there is the chance that he will have less goodness; if he is careful about his religious duties, there is the chance he is behindhand in general knowledge; and in matter of fact, in particular cases, persons may be found, correct and virtuous, who are heavy, narrowminded, and unin-

tellectual, and again, unprincipled men, who are
brilliant and amusing. And thus you see, my
Brethren, how that particular temptation comes
about, of which I speak, when boyhood is past,
and youth is opening;—not only is the soul
plagued and tormented by the thousand temptations which rise up within it, but it is exposed
moreover to this sophistry of the Evil One,
whispering that duty and religion are very right
indeed, admirable, supernatural,—who doubts it?
—but that, somehow or other, religious people are
commonly either very dull or very tiresome: nay,
that religion itself after all is more suitable to women and children, who live at home, than to men.

O my Brethren, do you not confess to the
truth of much of what I have been saying? Is
it not so, that, when your mind began to open,
in proportion as it opened, it was by that very
opening made rebellious against what you knew
to be duty? In matter of fact, was not your
intellect in league with disobedience? Instead
of uniting knowledge and religion, as you might
have done, did you not set one against the
other? For instance, was it not one of the first
voluntary exercises of your mind, to indulge a
wrong curiosity?—a curiosity which you con-

fessed to yourselves to be wrong, which went against your conscience, while you indulged it. You desired to know a number of things, which it could do you no good to know. This is how boys begin; as soon as their mind begins to stir, it looks the wrong way, and runs upon what is evil. This is their first wrong step; and their next use of their intellect is to put what is evil into words: this is their second wrong step. They form images, and entertain thoughts, which should be away, and they stamp them upon themselves and others by expressing them. And next, the bad turn which they do to others, others retaliate on them. One wrong speech provokes another; and thus there grows up among them from boyhood that miserable tone of conversation,—hinting and suggesting evil, jesting, bantering on the subject of sin, supplying fuel for the inflammable imagination,—which lasts through life, which is wherever the world is, which is the very breath of the world, which the world cannot do without, which the world "speaks out of the abundance of its heart", and which you may prophesy will prevail in every ordinary assemblage of men, as soon as they are at their ease and begin to talk freely,—a sort of vocal worship of the Evil One, to which the Evil One listens with special satisfaction, because he looks on it as the preparation for worse sin; for from bad thoughts and bad words proceed bad deeds.

Bad company creates a distaste for good; and hence it happens that, when a youth has gone the length I have been supposing, he is repelled, from that very distaste, from those places and scenes which would do him good. He begins to lose the delight he once had in going home. By little and little he loses his enjoyment in the pleasant countenances, and untroubled smiles, and gentle ways, of that family circle which is so dear to him still. At first he says to himself that he is not worthy of them, and therefore keeps away; but at length the routine of home is tiresome to him. He has aspirations and ambitions which home does not satisfy. He wants more than home can give. His curiosity now takes a new turn; he listens to views and discussions which are inconsistent with the sanctity of religious faith. At first he has no temptation to adopt them; only he wishes to know what is "said". As time goes on, however, living with companions who have no fixed principle, and

who, if they do not oppose, at least do not take
for granted, any the most elementary truths, or
worse, hearing or reading what is directly
against religion, at length, without being conscious of it, he admits a sceptical influence upon
his mind. He does not know it, he does not recognize it, but there it is; and, *before* he recognizes it, it leads him to a fretful impatient way
of speaking of the persons, conduct, words, and
measures of religious men or of men in authority.
This is the way in which he relieves his mind of
the burden which is growing heavier and heavier
every day. And so he goes on, approximating
more and more closely to sceptics and infidels,
and feeling more and more congeniality with
their modes of thinking, till some day suddenly,
from some accident, the fact breaks upon him, and
he sees clearly that he is an unbeliever himself.

He can no longer conceal from himself that
he does not believe, and a sharp anguish darts
through him, and for a time he is made miserable; next, he *laments* indeed that former un-
doubting faith, which he has lost, but as some
pleasant dream;—a dream, though a pleasant
one, from which he has been awakened, but
which, however pleasant, *he*, forsooth, cannot

help *being* a dream. And his next stage is to
experience a great expansion and elevation of
mind; for his field of view is swept clear of all
that filled it from childhood, and now he may
build up for himself anything he pleases instead.
So he begins to form his own ideas of things, and
these please and satisfy him for a time; then he
gets used to them, and tires of them, and he takes
up others; and now he has begun that everlasting round of seeking and never finding: at
length, after various trials, he gives up the search
altogether, and decides that nothing can be
known, and there is no such thing as truth, and
that if anything is to be professed, the creed he
started from is as good as any other, and has
more claims;—however, that really nothing is
true, nothing is certain. Or, if he be of a more
ardent temperature, or, like Augustine, the object of God's special mercy, then he cannot give
up the inquiry, though he has no chance of solving it, and he roams about, "walking through
dry places, seeking rest, and finding none". Meanwhile poor Monica sees the change in its effects,
though she does not estimate it in itself, or know
exactly what it is, or how it came about: nor,
even though it be told her, can she enter in it,

or understand how one, so dear to her, can be subjected to it. But a dreadful change there is, and she perceives it too clearly; a dreadful change for him and for her; a wall of separation has grown up between them: she cannot throw it down again: but she can turn to her God, and weep and pray.

Now, my Brethren, observe, the strength of this delusion lies in there being a sort of truth in it. Young men feel a consciousness of certain faculties within them, which demand exercise, aspirations which must have an object, for which they do not commonly find exercise or object in religious circles. This want is no excuse for them, if they think, say, or do anything against faith or morals; but still it is the occasion of their sinning. It is the fact, they are not only moral, they are intellectual beings; but, ever since the fall of man, religion is here, and philosophy is there; each has its own centres of influence, separate from the other; intellectual men desiderate something in the homes of religion, and religious men desiderate something in the schools of science.

Here, then, I conceive, is the object of the Holy See and the Catholic Church in setting up

Universities; it is to reunite things which were in the beginning joined together by God, and have been put asunder by man. Some persons will say that I am thinking of confining, distorting, and stunting the growth of the intellect by ecclesiastical supervision. I have no such thought. Nor have I any thought of a compromise, as if religion must give up something, and science something. I wish the intellect to range with the utmost freedom, and religion to enjoy an equal freedom; but what I am stipulating for is, that they should be found in one and the same place, and exemplified in the same persons. I want to destroy that diversity of centres, which puts everything into confusion by creating a contrariety of influences. I wish the same spots and the same individuals to be at once oracles of philosophy and shrines of devotion. It will not satisfy me, what satisfies so many, to have two independent systems, intellectual and religious, going at once side by side, by a sort of division of labour, and only accidentally brought together. It will not satisfy me, if religion is here, and science there, and young men converse with science all day, and lodge with religion in the evening. It is not touching the evil, to which these remarks have been directed, if young men eat and drink and sleep in one place, and think in another: I want the same roof to contain both the intellectual and moral discipline. Devotion is not a sort of finish given to the sciences; nor is science a sort of feather in the cap, if I may dare so to express myself, an ornament and set-off of devotion. I want the intellectual layman to be religious, and the devout ecclesiastic to be intellectual.

This is no matter of terms, nor of subtle distinctions. Sanctity has its influence; intellect has its influence; the influence of sanctity is the greater on the long run; the influence of intellect is the greater at the moment. Therefore, in the case of the young, whose education lasts a few years, where the intellect is, *there* is the influence. Their literary, their scientific teachers really have the forming of them. Let both influences act freely, and then, as a general rule, no system of mere religious guardianship which neglects the Reason, will in matter of fact succeed against the School. Youths need a masculine religion, if it is to carry captive their restless imaginations, and their wild intellects, as well as to touch their susceptible hearts.

Look down then upon us from heaven, O blessed Monica, for we are engaged in supplying that very want which called for thy prayers, and gained for thee thy crown. Thou who didst obtain thy son's conversion by the merit of thy intercession, continue that intercession for us, that we may be blest, as human instruments, in the use of those human means by which ordinarily the Holy Cross is raised aloft, and religion commands the world. Gain for us, first, that we may intensely feel that God's grace is all in all, and that we are nothing; next, that, for His greater glory, and for the honour of Holy Church, and for the good of man, we may be "zealous for all the better gifts", and may excel in intellect as we excel in virtue.

SERMON II.

THE RELIGION OF THE PHARISEE, THE RELIGION OF MANKIND.

Evang. Sec. Luc., c. xviii. v. 13.
Deus propitius esto mihi peccatori.
O God, be merciful to me, a sinner.

THESE words set before us what may be called the characteristic mark of the Christian Religion, as contrasted with the various forms of worship and schools of belief, which in early or in later times have spread over the earth. They are a confession of sin and a prayer for mercy. Not indeed that the notion of transgression and of forgiveness was introduced by Christianity, and is unknown beyond its pale; on the contrary, most observable it is, the symbols of guilt and pollution, and rites of deprecation and expiation, are more or less common to them all; but what is peculiar to our divine faith, as to Judaism before it, is this, that confession of sin enters into the idea of its highest saintliness, and that its pattern worshippers and the very heroes of its history are only, and can only be, and cherish in their hearts the everlasting memory that they are, and carry with them into heaven the rapturous avowal of their being, redeemed, restored transgressors. Such an avowal is not simply wrung from the lips of the neophyte, or of the lapsed; it is not the cry of the common run of men alone, who are buffeting with the surge of temptation in the wide world; it is the hymn of saints, it is the triumphant ode sounding from the heavenly harps of the Blessed before the Throne, who sing to their Divine Redeemer, "Thou wast slain, and hast redeemed us to God in Thy blood, out of every tribe, and tongue, and people, and nation".

And what is to the saints above a theme of never-ending thankfulness, is, while they are yet on earth, the matter of their perpetual humiliation. Whatever be their advance in the spiritual life, they never rise from their knees, they never cease to beat their breasts, as if sin could possibly be strange to them while they were in the flesh. Even our Lord Himself, the very Son of God in human nature, and infinitely separate from sin,—even His Immaculate Mother, encompassed by His grace from the first beginnings of her existence, and without any part of the original stain,—even they, as descended from Adam, were subjected at least to death, the direct, emphatic punishment of sin. And much more, even the most favoured of that glorious company, whom He has washed clean in His Blood; they never forget what they were by birth; they confess, one and all, that they are children of Adam, and of the same nature as their brethren, and compassed with infirmities while in the flesh, whatever may be the grace given them and their own improvement of it. Others may look up to them, but they ever look up to God; others may speak of their merits, but they only speak of their defects. The young and unspotted, the aged and most mature, he who has sinned least, he who has repented most, the fresh innocent brow, and the hoary head, they unite in this one litany, "O God, be merciful to me, a sinner". So was it with St. Aloysius; so, on the other hand, was it with St. Ignatius; so was it with St. Rose, the youngest of the saints, who, as a child, submitted her tender frame to the most amazing penances; so was it with St.

Philip Neri, one of the most aged, who, when some one praised him, cried out, " Begone! I am a devil, and not a saint"; and, when going to communicate, would protest before his Lord, that he " was good for nothing, but to do evil". Such utter self-prostration, I say, is the very badge and token of the servant of Christ;—and this indeed is conveyed in His own words, when He says, " I am not come to call the just, but sinners"; and it is solemnly recognized and inculcated by Him, in the words which follow the text, " Every one that exalteth himself, shall be humbled, and he that humbleth himself, shall be exalted".

This, you see, my Brethren, is very different from that merely general acknowledgment of human guilt, and of the need of expiation, contained in those old and popular religions, which have before now occupied, or still occupy, the world. In them, guilt is an attribute of individuals, or of particular places, or of particular acts of nations, of body politics or their rulers, for whom, in consequence, purification is necessary. Or it is the purification of the worshipper, not so much personal as ritual, before he makes his offering, and an act of introduction to his religious service. All such practices indeed are remnants of true religion, and tokens and witnesses of it, useful both in themselves and in their import; but they do not rise to the explicitness and the fulness of the Christian doctrine. "There is not any man just". "All have sinned, and do need the glory of God". "Not by the works of justice, which we have done, but according to His mercy". The disciples of other worships and other philosophies thought and think, that the many indeed are bad, but the few are good. As their thoughts passed on from the ignorant and erring multitude to the select specimens of mankind, they left the notion of guilt behind, and they pictured for themselves an idea of truth and wisdom, perfect, indefectible, and self-sufficient. It was a sort of virtue without imperfection, which took pleasure in contemplating itself, which needed nothing, and which was, from its own internal excellence, sure of a reward. Their descriptions, their stories of good and religious men, are often beautiful, and admit of an instructive interpretation; but in themselves they have this great blot, that they make no mention of sin, and that they speak as if that shame and humiliation were no properties of the virtuous. I will remind you, my Brethren, of a very beautiful story, which you have read in a writer of antiquity; and the more beautiful it is, the more it is fitted for my present purpose, for the defect in it will come out the more strongly by the very contrast, viz., the defect that, though in some sense it teaches piety, humility it does not teach. I say, when the Psalmist would describe the happy man, he says: "Blessed are they whose iniquities are forgiven, and whose sins are covered; blessed is the man to whom the Lord hath not imputed sin". Such is the blessedness of the Gospel; but what is the blessedness of the religions of the world? A celebrated Greek sage once paid a visit to a prosperous king of Lydia, who, after showing him all his greatness and his glory, asked him whom he considered to have the happiest lot, of all men whom he had known. On this the philosopher, passing by the monarch himself, named a countryman of his own, as fulfilling his typical idea of human perfection. The most blessed of men, he said, was Tellus of Athens, for he lived in a flourishing city, and was prospered in his children, and in their families; and then at length, when war ensued with a border state, he took his place in the battle, repelled the enemy, and died gloriously, being buried at the public expense where he fell, and receiving public honours. When the king asked who came next to him in Solon's judgment, the sage went on to name two brothers, conquerors at the games, who, when the oxen were not forthcoming, drew their mother, who was priestess, to the temple, to the great admiration of the assembled multitude; and who, on her praying for them the best of possible rewards, after sacrificing and feasting, lay down to sleep in the temple, and never rose again. No one can deny the beauty of these pictures; but it is for that reason I select them; they are the pictures of men who were not supposed to have any grave account to settle with heaven, who had easy duties, as they thought, and who fulfilled them.

Now perhaps you will ask me, my Brethren, whether this heathen idea of religion be not really higher than that which I have called preëminently Christian; for surely to obey in simple tranquillity and unsolicitous confidence, is the noblest conceivable state of the creature, and the most acceptable worship he can pay to the Creator. Doubtless it is the noblest and most acceptable worship; such has ever been the worship of the angels; such is the worship now of the spirits of the just made perfect; such will be the worship of the whole company of the glorified after the general resurrection. But we are engaged in considering the actual state of man, as found in this world; and I say, considering what he is, any standard of duty, which does not convict him of real and multiplied sins, and of incapacity to please God of his own strength, is untrue; and any rule of life, which leaves him contented with himself, without fear, without anxiety, without humiliation, is deceptive; it is the blind leading the blind: yet such, in one shape or other, is the religion of the whole earth, beyond the pale of the Church.

The natural conscience of man, if cultivated from within, if enlightened by those external aids which in varying degrees are given him in every place and time, would teach him much of his duty to God and man, and would lead him on, by the guidance both of Providence and grace, into the fulness of religious knowledge; but, generally speaking, he is contented that it should tell him very little, and he makes no efforts to gain any juster views than he has at first, of his relations to the world around him and to his Creator. Thus he apprehends part, and part only, of the moral law; has scarcely any idea at all of sanctity; and, instead of tracing actions to their source, which is the motive, and judging them thereby, he measures them for the most part by their effects and their outward aspect. Such is the way with the multitude of men every where and at all times; they do not set the Image of Almighty God before them, and ask themselves what He wishes: if once they did this, they would begin to see how much He requires, and they would earnestly come to Him, both to be pardoned for what they do wrong, and for the power to do better. And, for the same reason that they do not please Him, they succeed in pleasing themselves. For that contracted, defective range of duties, which falls so short of God's law, is just what they can fulfil; or rather they choose it, and keep to it, *because* they can fulfil it. Hence, they become both self-satisfied and self-sufficient;—they think they know just what they ought to do, and that they do it all; and in consequence they are very well content with themselves, and rate their merit very high, and have no fear at all of any future scrutiny into their conduct, which may befall them, though their religion mainly lies in certain outward observances, and not a great number even of them.

So it was with the Pharisee in this day's gospel. He looked upon himself with great complacency, for the very reason that the standard was so low, and the range so narrow, which he assigned to his duties towards God and man. He used, or misused, the traditions in which he had been brought up, to the purpose of persuading himself, that perfection lay in merely answering the demands of society. He professed, indeed, to pay thanks to God, but he hardly apprehended the existence of any direct duties on his part towards his Maker. He thought he did all that God required, if he satisfied public opinion. To be religious, in the Pharisee's sense, was to keep the peace towards others, to take his share in the burdens of the poor, to abstain from gross vice, and to set a good example. His alms and fastings were not done in penance, but because the world asked for them; penance would have implied the consciousness of sin; whereas it was only Publicans, and such as they, who had anything to be forgiven. And these indeed were the outcasts of society, and despicable; but no account lay against men of well-regulated minds, such as his: men who were well-behaved, decorous, consistent, and respectable. He thanked God he was a Pharisee, and not a penitent.

Such was the Jew in our Lord's day; and such the heathen was, and had been. Alas! I do not mean to affirm that it was common for the poor heathen to observe even any religious rule at all; but I am speaking of the few and of the better sort: and these, I say, commonly took up with a religion like the Pharisee's, more beautiful perhaps and more poetical, but not at all deeper or truer than his. They did not indeed fast, or give alms, or observe the ordinances of Judaism; they threw over their meagre observances a philosophical garb, and embellished them with the refinements of a cultivated intellect; still their notion of moral and religious duty was as shallow as that of the Pharisee, and the sense of sin, the habit of self-abasement, and the desire of contrition, just as absent from their minds as from his. They framed a code of morals which they could without trouble obey; and then they were content with it and with themselves. Virtue, according to Xenophon, one of the best principled and most religious of their writers, and one who had seen a great deal of the world, and had the opportunity of bringing together in one the highest thoughts of many schools and countries,—virtue, according to him, consists mainly in command of the appetites and passions, and in serving others in order that they may serve us. He says, in the well known Fable, called the Choice of Hercules, that Vice has no real enjoyment even of those pleasures which it aims at; that it eats before it is hungry, and drinks before it is thirsty, and slumbers before it is wearied. It never hears, he says, that sweetest of voices, its own praise; it never sees that greatest luxury among sights, its own good deeds. It enfeebles the bodily frame of the young, and the intellect of the old. Virtue, on the other hand, rewards young men with the praise of their elders, and it rewards the aged with the reverence of youth; it supplies them pleasant memories and present peace; it secures the favour of heaven, the love of friends, a country's thanks, and, when death comes, an everlasting renown. In all such descriptions, virtue is something external; it is not concerned with motives or intentions; it is occupied in deeds which bear upon society, and which gain the praise of men; it has little to do with conscience and the Lord of conscience; and knows nothing of shame, humiliation, and penance. It is in substance the Pharisee's religion, though it be more graceful and more interesting.

Now this age is as removed in distance, as in character, from that of the Greek philosopher; yet who will say that the religion which it acts upon is very different from the religion of the heathen? Of course I understand well, that it might know, and that it will say, a great many things foreign and contrary to heathenism. I am well aware that the theology of this age is very different from what it was two thousand years ago. I know men profess a great deal, and boast that they are Christians, and speak of Christianity as being a religion of the heart; but, when we put aside words and professions, and try to discover what their religion is, we shall find, I fear, that the great mass of men in fact get rid of all religion that is inward; that they lay no stress on acts of faith, hope, and charity, on simplicity of intention, purity of motive, or mortification of the thoughts; that they confine themselves to two or three virtues, superficially practised; that they know not the words contrition, penance, and pardon; and that they think and argue that, after all, if a man does his duty in the world, according to his vocation, he cannot fail to go to heaven, however little he may do besides, nay, however much, in other matters, he may do that is undeniably unlawful. Thus a soldier's duty is loyalty, obedience, and valour, and he may let other matters take their chance; a trader's duty is honesty; an artizan's duty is industry and contentment; of a gentleman are required veracity, courteousness, and self-respect; of a public man, high-principled ambition; of a woman, the domestic virtues; of a minister of religion, decorum, benevolence, and some activity. Now, all these are instances of mere Pharisaical excellence; because there is no apprehension of Almighty God, no insight into His claims on us, no sense of the creature's short-comings, no self-condemnation, confession, and deprecation, nothing of those deep and sacred feelings which ever characterize the religion of a Christian, and more and more, not less and less, as he mounts up from mere ordinary obedience to the perfection of a saint.

And such, I say, is the religion of the natural man in every age and place;—often very beautiful on the surface, but worthless in God's sight;

good, as far as it goes, but worthless and hopeless, because it does not go further, because it is based on self-sufficiency, and results in self-satisfaction. I grant, it may be beautiful to look at, as in the instance of the young ruler whom our Lord looked at and loved, yet sent away sad; it may have all the delicacy, the amiableness, the tenderness, the religious sentiment, the kindness, which is actually seen in many a father of a family, many a mother, many a daughter, in the length and breadth of these kingdoms, in a refined and polished age like this; but still it is rejected by the heart-searching God, because all such persons walk by their own light, not by the True Light of men, because self is their supreme teacher, and because they pace round and round in the small circle of their own thoughts and of their own judgments, careless to know what God says to them, and fearless of being condemned by Him, if only they stand approved in their own sight. And thus they incur the force of those terrible words, spoken not to a Jewish ruler, nor to a heathen philosopher, but to a fallen Christian community, to the Christian Pharisees of Laodicea,—" Because thou sayest I am rich, and made wealthy, and have need of nothing; and knowest not that thou art wretched, and miserable, and poor, and blind, and naked; I counsel thee to buy of Me gold fire-tried, that thou mayest be made rich, and be clothed in white garments, that 'thy shame may not appear, and anoint thine eyes with eye-salve, that thou mayest see. Such as I love, I rebuke and chastise; be zealous, therefore, and do penance".

Yes, my Brethren, it is the ignorance of our understanding, it is our spiritual blindness, it is our banishment from the presence of Him who is the source and the standard of all Truth, which is the cause of this meagre, heartless religion of which men are commonly so proud. Had we any proper insight into things as they are, had we any real apprehension of God as He is, of ourselves as we are, we should never dare to serve Him without fear, or to rejoice unto Him without trembling. And it is the removal of this veil which is spread between our eyes and heaven, it is the pouring in upon the soul of the illuminating grace of the New Covenant, which makes the religion of the Christian so different from that of the various human rites and philosophies, which are spread over the earth. The Catholic saints alone confess sin, because the Catholic saints alone see God. That awful Creator Spirit, of whom the Epistle of this day speaks so much, He it is who brings into religion the true devotion, the true worship, and changes the self-satisfied Pharisee into the broken-hearted, self-abased Publican. It is the sight of God, revealed to the eye of faith, that makes us hideous to ourselves, from the contrast which we find ourselves to present to that great God at whom we look. It is the vision of Him in His infinite gloriousness, the All-holy, the All-beautiful, the All-perfect, which makes us sink into the earth with self-contempt and self-abhorrence. We are contented with ourselves till we contemplate Him. Why is it, I say, that the moral code of the world is so precise and well-defined? Why is the worship of reason so calm? Why was the religion of classic heathenism so joyous? Why is the framework of civilized society all so graceful and so correct? Why, on the other hand, is there so much of emotion, so much of conflicting and alternating feeling, so much that is high, so much that is abased, in the devotion of Christianity? It is because the Christian, and the Christian alone, has a revelation of God; it is because he has upon his mind, in his heart, on his conscience, the idea of One who is Self-dependent, who is from Everlasting, who is Incommunicable. He knows that One alone is holy, and that His own creatures are so frail in comparison of Him, that they would dwindle and melt away in His presence, did He not uphold them by His power. He knows that there is One whose greatness and whose blessedness are not affected, the centre of whose stability is not moved, by the presence or the absence of the whole creation with its innumerable beings and portions; whom nothing can touch, nothing can increase or diminish; who was as mighty before He made the worlds as since, and as serene and blissful since He made them as before. He knows that there is just One Being, in whose hand lies his own happiness, his own sanctity, his own life, and hope, and salvation. He knows that there is One to whom he owes everything, and against whom he can have no plea or remedy. All things are nothing before Him; the highest beings do but worship Him the more; the holiest beings are such, only because they have a greater portion of Him.

Ah! what has he to pride in now, when he looks back upon himself? Where has fled all that comeliness which heretofore he thought embellished him? What is he but some vile reptile, which ought to shrink aside out of the light of day? This was the feeling of St. Peter, when he first gained a glimpse of the greatness of his Master, and cried out, almost beside himself: "Depart from me, for I am a sinful man, O Lord!" It was the feeling of Holy Job, though he had served God for so many years, and had been so perfected in virtue, when the Almighty answered him from the whirlwind: "With the hearing of the ear I have heard Thee", he said; "but now my eye seeth Thee; therefore I reprove myself, and do penance in dust and ashes". So was it with Isaias, when he saw the vision of the Seraphim, and said: "Woe is me .. I am a man of unclean lips, and I dwell in the midst of a people that hath unclean lips, and I have seen with my eyes the King, the Lord of hosts". So was it with Daniel, when, even at the sight of an Angel, sent from God, "there remained no strength in him, but the appearance of his countenance was changed in him, and he fainted away, and retained no strength". This, then, my Brethren, is the reason why every son of man, whatever be his degree of holiness, whether a returning prodigal or a matured saint, says with the Publican, "O God, be merciful to me"; it is because created natures, high and low, are all on a level in the sight and in comparison of the Creator, and so all of them have one speech, and one only, whether he be the thief on the cross, Magdalen at the feast, or St. Paul before his martyrdom:—not that one of them may not have, what another has not, but that one and all have nothing but what comes from Him, and are as nothing before Him, who is all in all.

For us, my dear Brethren, whose duties lie in this seat of learning and science, may we never be carried away by any undue fondness for any human branch of study, so as to be forgetful that our true wisdom, and nobility, and strength, consist in the knowledge of Almighty God. Nature and man are our studies, but God is higher than all. It is easy to lose Him in His works. It is easy to become over-attached to our own pursuit, to substitute it for religion, and to make it the fuel of pride. Our secular attainments will avail us nothing, if they be not subordinate to religion. The knowledge of the sun, moon, and stars, of the earth and its three kingdoms, of the classics, or of history, will never bring us to heaven. We may thank God, that we are not as the illiterate and the dull; and those whom we despise, if they do but know how to ask mercy of Him, know what is very much more to the purpose of getting to heaven, than all our letters and all our science. Let this be the spirit in which we end our Session. Let us thank Him for all that He has done for us, for what He is doing by us; but let nothing that we know or that we can do, keep us from a personal, individual adoption of the great Apostle's words, "Christ Jesus came into this world to save sinners, of whom I am the chief".

SERMON III.

WAITING FOR CHRIST.

Ep. I. Paul ad Thessal., c. i. v. 9, 10.

Servire Deo vivo et vero, et expectare Filium ejus de cœlis, quem suscitavit ex mortuis, Jesum, qui eripuit nos ab irâ venturâ.

To serve the Living and True God, and to wait for His Son from heaven, whom He raised from the dead, Jesus, who hath delivered us from the wrath to come.

As we approach the season of our Lord's advent, we are warned Sunday after Sunday by our tender Mother, Holy Church, of the duty of looking out for it. Last week we were reminded of that dreadful day, when the Angels shall reap the earth, and gather together the noxious weeds out of the midst of the corn, and bind them in bundles for the burning. Next week we shall read of that "great tribulation", which will immediately precede the failing of

sun and moon, and the appearance of the Sign
of the Son of man in heaven. And to-day
we are told to wait in expectation of that awful
Sign, serving the Living and True God the
while, as is His due, who has "converted us
from idols" and "delivered us from the wrath to
come".

What St. Paul calls "waiting", or "expecting",
or "looking out", that our Lord Himself enjoins
upon us, when he bids us "look up and lift up our
heads, when these things begin to come to pass";
as if it were our duty to be on the alert, starting
up at the first notice, and straining, as it were,
our eyes with eager and devout interest, that
we may catch the earliest sight of His presence,
when He is manifested in the heavens—just as a
whole city or country from time to time is found
to sit up all night for the appearance of some meteor or strange star, which Science has told them
is to come. Elsewhere, this frame of mind is called
watching,—whether by our Lord or by His holy
Apostles after Him. "Watch ye, therefore", He
says Himself, "for you know not when the Lord
of the house cometh; at even, or at midnight, or
at the cock-crowing, or in the morning; lest,
coming suddenly, He find you sleeping. And

what I say to you, I say to all,—Watch". And St. Paul: "It is now the hour for us to rise from sleep; for now our salvation is nearer than when we believed. The night is past, the day is at hand". And St. John: "Behold, I come as a thief. Blessed is he that watcheth and keepeth his garments".

Passages such as these might be multiplied, and they lead to reflections of various kinds. The substance of religion consists in faith, hope, and charity; and the qualification for eternal life is to be in a state of grace and free from mortal sin; yet, when we come to the question, how we are to preserve ourselves in a state of grace, and gain the gift of perseverance in it, then a number of observances have claims upon us, over and above those duties in which the substance of religion lies, as being its safeguard and protection. And these same observances, as being of a nature to catch the eye of the world, become the badges of the Christian, as contrasted with other men; whereas faith, hope, and charity are lodged deep in the breast, and are not seen. Now, one of these characteristics of a Christian spirit, springing from the three theological virtues, and then in turn defending and strengthening them, is that habit of waiting and watching, to which this season of the year especially invites us; and the same habit is also a mark of the children of the Church, and a note of her divine origin.

If, indeed, we listen to the world, we shall take another course. We shall think the temper of mind I am speaking of, to be superfluous or enthusiastic. We shall aim at doing only what is necessary, and shall try to find out how little will be enough. We shall look out, not for Christ, but for the prizes of this life. We shall form our judgment of things by what others say; we shall admire what they admire; we shall instinctively reverence and make much of the world's opinion. We shall fear to give scandal to the world. We shall have a secret shrinking from the Church's teaching. We shall have an uneasy, uncomfortable feeling when mention is made of the maxims of holy men and ascetical writers, not liking them, yet not daring to dissent. We shall be scanty in supernatural acts, and have little or nothing of the habits of virtue which are formed by them, and are an armour of proof against temptation. We shall suffer our souls to be overrun with venial sins, which tend to mortal sin, if they have not already reached it. We shall feel very reluctant to face the thought of death. All this shall we be, all this shall we do; and in consequence, it will be very difficult for a spectator to say how we differ from respectable, well-conducted men who are not Catholics. In that case certainly we shall exhibit no pattern of a Christian spirit, nor shall we be in our own persons any argument for the truth of Christianity; but I am trusting and supposing that our view of Christianity is higher than to be satisfied with conduct so unlike that to which our Saviour and His Apostles call us.

Speaking, then, to men who wish now to take that side and that place which they will have wished to have taken when their Lord actually comes to them, I say, that we must not only have faith in Him, but must wait on Him; not only must hope, but must watch for Him; not only love Him, but must long for Him; not only obey Him, but must look out, look up earnestly for our reward, which is Himself. We must not only make Him the Object of our faith, hope, and charity, but we must make it our duty not to believe the world, not to hope in the world, not to love the world. We must resolve not to hang on the world's opinion, or study its wishes. It is our mere wisdom to be thus detached from all things below. "The time is short", says the Apostle; "it remaineth that they who weep be as though they wept not, and they that rejoice as if they rejoiced not, and they that buy as though they possessed not, and they that use this world as if they used it not, for the fashion of this world passeth away".

We read in the Gospel of our Lord on one occasion "entering into a certain town", and being received and entertained "by a certain woman named Martha". There were two sisters, Martha and Mary; "Martha was busy about much serving"; but Mary sat at our Lord's feet, and heard His words. You recollect, my Brethren, His comparison of these two holy sisters, one with another. "Martha, Martha", He said, "thou art careful, and art troubled about many things, but one thing is necessary; Mary hath chosen the best part". Now, Martha loved Him, and Mary loved Him; but Mary waited on Him, too, and, therefore, had the promise of perseverance held up to her; "Mary hath chosen the best part, which shall not be taken away from her".

They, then, watch and wait for their Lord, who are tender and sensitive in their devotion towards Him; who feed on the thought of Him, hang on His words, live in His smile, and thrive and grow under His hand. They are eager for His approval, quick in catching His meaning, jealous of His honour. They see Him in all things, expect Him in all events; and, amid all the cares, the interests, and the pursuits of this life, still would feel an awful joy, not a disappointment, did they hear that He was on the point of coming. "By night I sought Him whom my soul loveth", says the inspired canticle; "I sought Him, and found Him out. I will rise, and in the streets and broad places will I seek Him". Must I be more definite in my description of this affectionate temper? I ask, then, do you know the feeling of expecting a friend, expecting him to come, and he delays? or do you know what it is to be in the company of those with whom you are not at your ease, and to wish the time to pass away, and the hour to strike, when you are to be released from them? or do you know what it is to be in anxiety lest something should happen, which may happen, or may not; or to be in suspense about some important event, which makes your heart beat when anything reminds you of it, and of which you think the first thing in the morning? or do you know what it is to have friends in a distant country, to expect news from them, and to wonder from day to day what they are doing, and whether they are well? or do you know, on the other hand, what it is to be in a strange country yourself, with no one to talk to, no one who can sympathise with you, homesick,—downcast, because no letter comes to you,—and perplexed how you are ever to get back again? or do you know what it is so to love and live upon a person who is present with you, that your eyes follow his, that you read his soul, that you see its changes in his countenance, that you anticipate his wants, that you are sad in his sadness, troubled when he is vexed, restless when you cannot understand him, relieved, comforted, when you have cleared up the mystery?

This is a state of mind, when our Lord and Saviour is its Object, not intelligible, at first sight, to the world, not easy to nature, yet of so ordinary fulfilment in the Church in all ages, as to become the sign of the Presence of Him who is unseen, and to be a sort of note of the divinity of our religion. You know there are subtle instincts in the inferior animals, by which they apprehend the presence of things which man cannot discern, as atmospheric changes, or convulsions of the earth, or their natural enemies, whom yet they do not actually see; and we consider the uneasiness or the terror which they exhibit, to be a proof that there is something near them which is the object of the feeling, and is the evidence of its own reality. Well, in some such way the continuous watching and waiting for Christ, which Prophets, Apostles, and the Church built upon them, have manifested, age after age, is a demonstration that the Object of it is not a dream or a fancy, but really exists; in other words, that He lives still, that He has ever lived, who was once upon earth, who died, who disappeared, who said He would come again.

For centuries before He came on earth, prophet after prophet was upon his high tower, looking out for Him, through the thick night, and watching for the faintest glimmer of the dawn. "I will stand upon my watch", says one of them, "fix my feet upon the tower, and I will watch to see what will be said to me. For, as yet, the vision is far off, and it shall appear at the end, and shall not lie; if it make any delay, wait for it, for it shall surely come, and it shall not be slack". Another prophet says, "O God, my God, to Thee do I watch at break of day. For Thee my soul hath thirsted in a desert land, where there is no way nor water". And another, "To Thee have I lifted up my eyes, who dwellest in the heaven; as the eyes of servants on the hands of their masters, as the eyes of the handmaid towards her mistress". And another, "O that Thou wouldst rend the heavens, and come down!—the mountains would melt away at Thy presence. They would melt, as at the burning of fire; the waters would burn with fire. From the beginning of the world the eye hath not seen, O God, besides Thee, what things Thou hast prepared for them that wait on Thee". Now, if there were any men who had a right to be attached to this world, not detached from it, it was the ancient servants of God. This earth was given them as their portion and reward by the very word of the Most High. Our reward is future; the Jew was promised a temporal reward. Yet they put aside God's good gift for His better promise; they sacrificed possession to hope. They would be content with nothing short of the fruition of their Creator; they would watch for nothing else than the face of their Deliverer. If earth must be broken up, if the heavens must be rent, if the elements must melt, if the order of nature must be undone, in order to His appearing, let the ruin be, rather than they should be without Him. Such was the intense longing of the Jewish worshipper, looking out for that which was to come; and I say, that their very eagerness in watching, and patience in waiting, are of a nature to startle the world, and to impress upon it the claims of Christianity to be accepted as true; for their perseverance in looking out proves that there was something to look out for.

Nor were the Apostles, after our Lord had come and gone, behind the Prophets in the keenness of their apprehension, and the eagerness of their longing for Him. The miracle of patient waiting was continued. When He went up on high from Mount Olivet, they kept looking up into heaven; and it needed Angels to send them to their work, before they gave over. And ever after, still it was *Sursum corda* with them. "Our conversation is in heaven", says St. Paul; that is, our citizenship, and our social duties, our active life, our daily intercourse, is with the world unseen; "from whence, also, we look for the Saviour, the Lord Jesus Christ". And again, "If you be risen with Christ, seek the things that are above, where Christ is sitting at the right hand of God. Mind the things that are above, not the things that are upon the earth; for ye are dead, and your life is hid with Christ in God. When Christ shall appear, who is your life, then you also shall appear with Him in glory".

So vivid and continuous was this state of mind with the Apostles and their successors, that to the world they seemed expecting the immediate re-appearance of their Lord. "Behold, He cometh with the clouds", says St. John, "and every eye shall see Him, and they also that pierced Him. And all the tribes of the earth shall bewail themselves because of Him. He that giveth testimony of those things, saith, surely, I come quickly. Amen, come, Lord Jesus". They forgot the long lapse of time, as holy men may do in trance. They passed over in their minds the slow interval, as the eye may be carried on beyond a vast expanse of flat country, and see only the glorious clouds in the distant horizon. Accordingly, St. Peter had to explain the matter. "In the last day", he says, "shall come deceitful scoffers, saying, where is the promise of His coming? But of this one thing be not ignorant, my beloved, that one day with the Lord is as a thousand years, and a thousand years as one day. Seeing all these things are to be dissolved, what manner of people ought you to be, in holy conversation and godliness, *looking for and waiting* unto the coming of the day of the Lord?" You see the great Apostle does not dissuade his brethren from anticipating the Day, while he confesses it will be long in coming. He explains the mistake of the world, which understood their eager expectation of our Lord's coming to be a proof that they thought that He was to come in their day; but how intense and absorbing must have been their thought of Him, that it was so mistaken! Nay, it is almost the description which St. Paul gives of the elect of God. When he was in prison, on the eve of his martyrdom, he sent to his beloved disciple, St. Timothy, his last words; and he says: "There is laid up for me a crown of justice; and not only to me, but"—to whom? how does he describe the heirs of glory? he proceeds, "not only to me, but to those also who *love His coming*".

This energetic, direct apprehension of an unseen Lord and Saviour has not been peculiar to Prophets and Apostles; it has been the habit of His Holy Church, and of her children, down to this day. Age passes after age, and she varies her discipline, and she adds to her devotions, and all with the one purpose, of fixing her own and their gaze more fully upon the person of her unseen Lord. She has adoringly surveyed Him, feature by feature, and has paid a separate homage to Him in every one. She has made us honour His Five Wounds, His Precious Blood, and His Sacred Heart. She has bid us meditate on His infancy, and the acts of His ministry; His agony, His scourging, and His crucifixion. She has sent us on pilgrimage to His birthplace and His sepulchre, and the mount of His ascension. She has sought out, and placed before us, the memorials of His life and death; His crib and holy house, His holy tunic, the handkerchief of St. Veronica, the cross and its nails, His winding-sheet, and the napkin for His head.

And so, again, if the Church has exalted Mary Joseph, it has been with a view to the glory of His sacred Humanity. If Mary is proclaimed as immaculate, it illustrates the doctrine of her Maternity. If she is called the Mother of God, it is to remind Him that, though He is out of sight, He, nevertheless, is our possession, for He is of the race of man. If she is painted with Him in her arms, it is because we will not suffer the Object of our love to cease to be human, because He is also divine. If she is the Mater Dolorosa, it is because she stands by His cross. If she is Maria Desolata, it is because His dead body is on her lap. If, again, she is the Coronata, the crown is set upon her head by His dear hand. And, in like manner, if we are devout to Joseph, it is as to His foster-father; and if he is the saint of happy death, it is because he dies in the hands of Jesus and Mary.

And what the Church urges on us down to this day, saints and holy men, down to this day, have exemplified. Is it necessary to refer to the lives of the Holy Virgins, who were and are His very spouses, wedded to Him by a mystical marriage, and in many instances visited here by the earnests of that ineffable celestial benediction which is in heaven their everlasting portion? The martyrs, the confessors of the Church, bishops, evangelists, doctors, preachers, monks, hermits, ascetical teachers,—have they not, one and all, as their histories show, lived on the very name of Jesus, as food, as medicine, as fragrance, as light, as life from the dead?—as one of them says, "in aure dulce canticum, in ore mel mirificum, in corde nectar cœlicum".

Nor is it necessary to be a saint thus to feel: this intimate, immediate dependence on Emmanuel, God with us, has been in all ages the characteristic, almost the definition, of a Christian. It is the ordinary feeling of Catholic populations; it is the elementary feeling of every one who has but a common hope of heaven. I recollect, years ago, hearing an acquaintance, not a Catholic, speak of a work of devotion, written as Catholics usually write, with wonder and perplexity, because (he said) the author wrote as if he had "a sort of personal attachment to our Lord"; "it was as if he had seen Him, known Him, lived with Him, instead of merely professing and believing the great doctrine of the Atonement". It is this same phenomenon which strikes those who are not Catholics, when they enter our churches. They themselves are accustomed to do religious acts simply as a duty;

they are serious at prayer time, and behave with decency, because it is a duty. But you know, my Brethren, mere duty, a sense of propriety, and good behaviour, these are not the ruling principles present in the minds of our worshippers. Wherefore, on the contrary, those spontaneous postures of devotion? why those unstudied gestures? why those abstracted countenances? why that heedlessness of the presence of others? why that absence of the shamefacedness which is so sovereign among professors of other creeds? The spectator sees the effect; he cannot understand the cause of it. *Why* is this simple earnestness of worship? *we* have no difficulty in answering. It is because the Incarnate Saviour is present in the tabernacle; and then, when suddenly the hitherto silent church is, as it were, illuminated with the full piercing burst of voices from the whole congregation, it is because He now has gone up upon His throne over the altar, there to be adored. It is the visible Sign of the Son of Man which thrills through the congregation, and makes them overflow with jubilation.

Here I am led to refer to a passage in the history of the last years of the wonderful man who swayed the destinies of Europe in the beginning of this century. It has before now attracted the attention of philosophers and preachers, as bearing on his sentiments towards Christianity, and containing an argument in its behalf cognate to that on which I have been insisting. It was an argument not unnatural in one who had that special passion for human glory, which has been the incentive of so many heroic careers and so many mighty revolutions in the history of the world. In the solitude of his imprisonment, and in the view of death, he is said to have expressed himself to the following effect:—

I have been accustomed to put before me the examples of Alexander and Cæsar, with the hope of rivalling their exploits, and living in the minds of men for ever. Yet, after all, in what sense does Cæsar, in what sense does Alexander live? Who knows or cares anything about them? At best, nothing but their names is known; for who among the multitude of men, who hear or who utter their names, really knows anything about their lives or their deeds, or attaches to those names any definite idea? Nay, even their names do but flit up and down the world like ghosts, mentioned only on particular occasions, or from accidental associations. Their chief home is the school-room; they have a foremost place in boys' grammars and exercise-books; they are splendid examples for themes; they form writing-copies. So low is heroic Alexander fallen, so low is imperial Cæsar; " ut pueris placeas et declamatio fias".

But, on the contrary (he is reported to have continued), there is just one Name in the whole world that lives; it is the Name of One who passed His years in obscurity, and who died a malefactor's death. Eighteen hundred years have gone since that time, but still It has Its hold upon the human mind. It has possessed the world, and It maintains possession. Amid the most various nations, under the most diversified circumstances, in the most cultivated, in the rudest, races and intellects, in all classes of society, the Owner of that great Name reigns. High and low, rich and poor, acknowledge Him. Millions of souls are conversing with Him, are venturing at His word, are looking for His presence. Palaces, sumptuous, innumerable, are raised to His honour; His image, in its deepest humiliation, is triumphantly displayed in the proud city, in the open country; at the corners of streets, on the tops of mountains. It sanctifies the ancestral hall, the closet, and the bedchamber; it is the subject for the exercise of the highest genius in the imitative arts. It is worn next the heart in life; it is held before the failing eyes in death. Here, then, is One who is not a mere name; He is not a mere fiction; He is a substance; He is dead and gone, but still He lives,—as the living, energetic thought of successive generations, and as the awful motive power of a thousand great events. He has done without effort, what others with lifelong, heroic struggles have not done. Can He be less than Divine? Who is He but the Creator Himself, who is sovereign over His own works; towards whom our eyes and hearts turn instinctively, because He is our Father and our God?

My Brethren, I have assumed that we are what we ought to be; but if there be any condition or description of men within the Church, who are in danger of failing in the duty on which I have been insisting, it is ourselves. If there be any who are not waiting on their Lord and Saviour, not keeping watch for Him, not longing for Him, not holding converse with Him, it is they who,

like ourselves, are in the possession, or in the
search, of temporal goods. Those saintly souls,
whose merits and satisfactions almost make them
sure of heaven, they, by the very nature of their
state, are living on Christ. Those holy communities of men and women, whose life is a mortification, they, by their very profession of perfection, are waiting and watching for Him. The
poor, those multitudes who pass their days in
constrained suffering, they, by the stern persuasion of that suffering, are looking out for Him.
But we, my Brethren, who are in easy circumstances, or in a whirl of business, or in a laby-
rinth of cares, or in a war of passions, or in the
race of wealth, or honour, or station, alas! we are
the very men who are likely to have no regard,
no hunger or thirst, no relish for the true bread
of heaven and the living water. "The Spirit
and the Bride say, come; and he that heareth,
let him say, come. And he that thirsteth, let
him come: and he that will, let him take of the
water of life, freely". God in His mercy rouse
our sluggish spirits, and inflame our earthly
hearts, that we may cease to be an exception in
His great family, which is ever adoring, praising,
and loving Him.

SERMON IV.

THE SECRET POWER OF DIVINE GRACE.

Evang. sec. Luc., c. xvii. v. 20, 21.

Non venit regnum Dei cum observatione: neque dicent, Ecce hic, aut ecce illic. Ecce enim regnum Dei intra vos est.

The kingdom of God cometh not with observation; neither shall they say, Behold here, or behold there. For lo, the kingdom of God is within you.

WHAT our Lord announces in these words, came to pass: and we commemorate it to this day, especially at this season of the year. The kingdom of God was inaugurated by the Apostles, and spread rapidly. It filled the world; it took possession of the high places of the earth; but it came and progressed without "observation". All other kingdoms that ever were, have sounded a trumpet before them, and have challenged attention. They have come out "with a sword, and with a spear, and with a shield". They have been the ravenous beast from the north, the swift eagle, or the swarming locusts. In the words of the Prophets, "Before them a devouring fire, and behind them a burning flame. The appearance of them has been as the appearance of horses, and they ran like horsemen... And the noise of their wings was as the noise of chariots and many horses running to battle". Such has ever been the coming of earthly power; and a Day will be, when that also will have a fulfilment and find its antitype in the history of heaven; for, when our Lord comes again, He too will come "with the word of command, and with the voice of an Archangel, and with the trumpet of God". This will be with observation; so will He end; so did He not begin His Church upon earth; for it had been foretold of Him, "He shall not contend, nor cry out; neither shall any man hear His voice in the streets. The bruised reed He shall not break, and smoking flax He shall not extinguish, till He send forth judgment unto victory".

And that noiseless, unostentatious conquest of the earth, made by the Holy Apostles of Christ, became, as regards the Jews, still more secret, from the circumstance that they believed it would be with outward show, though He assured them of the contrary. The Pharisees looked out for some sign from heaven. They would not believe that His kingdom could come, unless they saw it come; they looked out for a prince with troops in battle array; and since He came with twelve poor men and no visible pomp, He was to them as a "thief in the night", because of their incredulity, and He was come and in possession before they would allow that He was coming.

But the coming of His kingdom would any how have been secret, even though they had not been resolved that it should not be so. And He tells us in the text the reason why. "Neither shall they say, Behold here, or behold there. *For* lo, the kingdom of God is within you". You see, He tells us why He came so covertly. It could not be otherwise, because it was a conquest, not of the body, but of the heart. It was not an assault from without, but it was an inward influence, not subduing the outward man through the senses, but, in the words of the Apostle, " bringing into captivity every understanding unto the obedience of Christ". Kingdoms of this world spread in space and time;

they begin from a point, and they travel onwards, and range round. Their course may be traced: first they secure this territory, then they compass that. They make their ground good, as they go, and consolidate their power. Of course, the kingdom of Christ also, as being in this world, has an outward shape, and fortunes, and a history, like institutions of this world, though it be not *of* this world. It began from Jerusalem, and went forward to Scythia and to Africa, to India and to Britain; and it has ranks and officers and laws; it observes a strict discipline, and exacts an implicit obedience: but still this is not the full account, or the true process, of its rise and establishment. " The weapons of its warfare were not carnal"; it came by an inward and intimate visitation; by outward instruments, indeed, but with effects far higher than those instruments; with preaching and argument and discussion, but really by God's own agency. He who is Omnipotent and Omniscient, touched many hearts at once and in many places. They forthwith, one and all, spoke one language, not learning it one from the other, so much as taught by Himself the canticle of the Lamb; or, if by men's teaching too, yet catching and mastering it spontaneously, almost before the words were spoken. For time and space, cause and effect, are the servants of His will.

And so, voices broke out all at once into His praise, in the East and in the West, in the North and in the South: and the perplexed world searched about in vain, whence came that concord of sweet and holy sounds. Upon the first word of the preacher, upon a hint, upon a mere whisper in the air, a deep response came from many lips,—a deep, full, and ready harmony of many voices, one and all proclaiming the Saviour of men. For the Spirit of the Lord had descended and filled the earth; and there were thrilling hearts, and tremulous pulses, and eager eyes, in every place. It was a time of visitation, when the weak were to become strong, and the last become first. It was the triumph of faith, which delays not, but accepts generously and promptly, according to the Scripture, " The word is nigh thee, even in thy mouth and in thy heart; this is the word of faith, which we preach". And thus, as Nineveh and Babylon were surprised of old by the army of the enemy, so was the world thus surprised by Him, who, in prophetic language, rode upon a white horse, and was called "Faithful and True"; and, as it befell Egypt at the first Pasch, that there was not a house where there lay not one dead, so now, on this more gracious Passage, there was not a house where there was not one alive. For the Highest had come down among them, and was every where; the Lord of Angels was walking the earth; He was scattering His gifts freely, and multiplying His Image: and, in this sense, as well as in that in which He spoke the words, "a man's enemies were they of his own household". The despised, the hated influence insinuated itself every where; the leaven spread, and none could stay it; and in the most unlikely places, in the family of the haughty and fierce soldier, amid the superstitions of idolatry and the degradations of slavery, the noblest, and the ablest, and the fairest, as well as the brutish and the ignorant, one and all, by a secret power, become the prey of the Church and the bondsmen of Christ. And thus a great and wide-spreading kingdom flushed into existence all at once, like spring after winter, from within.

Such were the immediate concomitants of the first coming of Him, who was "the most abject of men", and "acquainted with infirmity", and whose "look was as it were hidden and despised", and "as one struck by God and afflicted". As the prophecy goes on to say, "He divided the spoil of the strong"; and, if you ask me, my Brethren, how it was that He did this marvel? what was the way and the instrument of His grace in His dealings with the spirits which He had created? I answer in brief, by referring back to the past history of our race. It is certain that man is not sufficient for his own happiness, that he is not himself, is not at home with himself, without the presence within him of the grace of Him who at that time has offered that grace to all freely. When he was created, then his Maker breathed into him the supernatural life of the Holy Spirit, which is his true happiness; when he fell, he forfeited the divine gift, and with it his happiness also. Ever since he has been unhappy; ever since he has felt a void in his breast, and does not know how to satisfy it. He scarcely apprehends his own need; only the unstudied, involuntary movements of his mind and heart show that he feels it, for he is either languid, dull, or apathetic under this hunger, or he is feverish and restless, seeking first in one thing, then in another, that blessing which he has lost. For a time, perhaps even till old age comes, he continues to form to himself some idol on which he may feed, and sustain some sort of existence, just as the weeds of the field or the innutritious earth may allay the pangs of famine. One man determines to rise in life, another is wrapt up in his family. Numbers get through the day and the year with the alternation of routine business and holyday recreation. Rich men are lavish in pomp and show; poor men give themselves to intemperance; the young give themselves up to sensual pleasures. They cannot live without an object of life, though it be an object unworthy of an immortal spirit.

Is it wonderful then, that, when the True Life, the very supply of the need of mankind, was again offered them in its fulness, that it should have carried power with it to persuade them to accept it? Is it wonderful that its announcement should have startled them, that its offer should have drawn them, that a first trial and a first fruit of the gift should have made them desirous of further and larger measures of it? This, then, is the secret of the triumph of the unearthly kingdom of God among the self-willed, self-wise children of Adam. Soldiers of this world receive their bounty-money on enlisting. They take it, and become the servants of an earthly prince: shall not they, much more, be faithful, yes, even unto the death, who have received the earnest of the true riches, who have been fed with "the hidden manna", who have, in the Apostle's words, "been once illuminated, and tasted the good word of God, and the powers of the world to come"? And thus it is that the kingdom of God spreads externally over the earth, because it has an internal hold upon us, because, in the words of the text, "it is within us", in the hearts of its individual members. Bystanders marvel; strangers try to analyse what it is that does the work; they imagine all manner of human reasons and natural causes, to account for it, because they cannot see, and do not feel, and will not believe, what is in truth a supernatural influence: and they impute to some caprice or waywardness of mind, or to the force of novelty, or to some mysterious, insidious persuasiveness, or to some foreign enemy, or to some dark and subtle plotting, and they view with alarm, and they fain would baffle, what is nothing else but the keen, vivid, constraining glance of Christ's countenance. "The Lord, turning, looked on Peter": and "as the lightning cometh out of the east, and appeareth even unto the west", such is the piercing, soul-subduing look of the Son of man. It is come, it is gone, it has done its work, its abiding work, and the world is at fault to account for it. It sees the result; it has not perceived, it has not eyes to see, the Divine Hand.

Nay, not the world only, but the Church herself, is oftentimes surprised, I may say even perplexed, at the operation of that grace which is without observation, and at the miraculous multiplication of her children. The net of Peter seems about to break, from the multitude of fishes, and is hard to draw to shore. So was it singularly in the first age, in the issues of that glorious history of primitive conversion on which I have been dwelling. "The Lord increased to the Church daily", says the text, "such as should be saved". This process went on for three centuries; then came a most bitter and horrible persecution; at length it ceased; and then with awful abruptness, rushing upon the wings of the wind, the overwhelming news was heard, that the Lord of the earth, the Roman Emperor, had become a Christian, and all his multitude of nations with him. What an announcement! no human hand did it—no human instrument of it, preacher or apologist, can be pointed out. It was not, " Behold here, or behold there"—it was the secret power of God acting directly without observation upon the hearts of men. All of a sudden, when least expected, in the deep night of persecution, " as a thief", He came. All of a sudden, the Rulers of the Church had upon their hands the gigantic task, to which she alone was equal, that of bringing into shape and consistency a whole world. The event, and the almost fearful grandeur of it, had been visibly described by prophecy a thousand years before it. " Lift up thy eyes round about", was the word of promise to the Church; " lift up thy eyes, and see. All these are gathered together, they are come to thee. Thou shalt be clothed with all these as with an ornament, and as a bride thou shalt put them about thee. The children of thy barrenness shall still say in thy ears, The place is too straight for me, make me room to dwell in. And thou shalt say in thy heart, Who hath begotten these? I was barren, and brought not forth, led away, and captive, and who hath brought up these? I was destitute and alone; and these, where were they? Thus saith the Lord God, Behold I will lift up My hand to the Gentiles, and will set up My standard to the people. And they shall bring thy sons in their arms, and carry thy daughters upon their shoulders. And kings shall be thy nursing fathers, and queens thy nurses. They shall worship thee with their face towards the earth, and they shall lick up the dust of thy feet".

My Brethren, you know our Lord spoke, when He went away, of coming back not only suddenly, but soon. Well, in the sense in which I have been describing, He is ever coming. Again and again He comes to His Church; He ever comes, as a strong warrior, bringing in with Him fresh and fresh captives of His arrows and his spear. That same marvel of an inward work in the souls of men on a large scale, which He wrought at the first, He is ever reiterating and renewing in the history of the Church down to this day. Multitudes are ever pouring into her, as the fish into Peter's net, beyond her own thought and her own act, by the immediate and secret operation of His grace. This is emphatically the case now. It is seen on a large scale all over Christendom. Fifty years ago religion seemed almost extinguished. To the eyes of man, it was simply declining and wasting away all through the last century. There were indeed in that century saints and doctors and zealous preachers and faithful populations, as heretofore, but these the world could not see. The political power and social influence of religion was ever less and less; and then at last a European revolution came, and in man's judgment all was lost. But in its deepest misfortunes began its most wonderful rise; a re-action set in, and steadily has it progressed with every sign of progress still. And in its progress the same phenomenon, I say, reveals itself, which we read of in the history of former times; for while the Holy Church has been praying and labouring on her own field, converts, beyond that field, whom she was not contemplating, have been added to her from all classes, as at the beginning. Germany and England, the special seats of her enemies, are the very scenes of this spontaneous accession. To the surprise of all that know them, often to their own surprise, those who fear the Church, or disown her doctrines, find themselves drawing near to her by some incomprehensible influence year after year, and at length give themselves up to her, and proclaim her sovereignty. Those who never spoke to a Catholic Priest, those who have never entered a Catholic Church, those even who have learned their religion from the Protestant Bible, have, in matter of fact, by the overruling Providence of God, been brought through that very reading to recognize the Mother of Saints. Her very name, her simple claim, constrains men to think of her, to inquire about her, to wish her to be what she says she is, to submit to her; not on any assignable reason, save the needs of human nature and the virtue of that grace, which works secretly, round about the Church, without observation.

My Brethren, there are those who imagine that, when we use great words of the Church, invest her with heavenly privileges, and apply to her the evangelical promises, we speak merely of some external and political structure. They think we mean to spend our devotion upon a human cause, and that we toil for an object of human ambition. They think that we should acknowledge, if cross-examined, that our ultimate purpose was the success of persons and parties, to whom we were bound in honour, or in interest, or in gratitude; and that, if we looked to objects above the world or beyond the grave, we did so with very secondary aims and faint perceptions. They fancy, as the largest concession of their liberality, that we are working from the desire, generous, but still human, of the praise of earthly superiors, and that, after all, in some way or other, we are living on the breath, and basking in the smile, of man. But the text, and the train of thought which I have been pursuing, remind us of the true view of the matter, were we ever likely to forget it. The Church is a collection of souls, brought together in one by God's secret grace, though that grace comes to them through visible instruments, and unites them to a visible hierarchy. What is seen, is not the whole of the Church, but the visible part of it. When we say that Christ loves His Church, we mean that He loves, nothing of earthly nature, but the fruit of His own grace;— the varied fruits of His grace in innumerable hearts, viewed as brought together in unity of faith and love and obedience, of sacraments, and doctrine, and order, and worship. The object which He contemplates, which He loves in the Church, is not human nature simply, but human nature illuminated and renovated by His own supernatural power. If He has called the visible Church His Spouse, it is because she is the special seat of this divine gift. If He loved Peter, it was not simply because he was His apostle, but because Peter had that intense, unearthly love of Him, and that faith which flesh and blood could not exercise, which were the fitting endowments of an apostle. If He loved John, it was not as merely one of the Twelve, but because he again was adorned with the special gift of supernatural chastity. If He loved Mary, Martha, and Lazarus, it was not only as His friends and guests, but for their burning charity, and their pure contrition, and their self-sacrificing devotion. So it is now: what He creates, what He contemplates, what He loves, what He rewards, is (in St. Peter's words) "the hidden man of the heart", of which the visible Church is the expression, the protection, the instrumental cause, and the outward perfection.

And therefore, applying this great truth to our own circumstances, let us ever bear in mind, my Brethren, that we in this place are only then really strong, when we are more than we seem to be. It is not our attainments or our talents, it is not philosophy or science, letters or arts, which will make us dear to God. It is not secular favour, or civil position, which can make us worthy the attention and the interest of the true Christian. A great University is a great power, and can do great things; but, unless it be something more than human, it is but foolishness and vanity in the sight and in comparison of the little ones of Christ. It is really dead, though it seems to live, unless it be grafted upon the True Vine, and is partaker of the secret supernatural life which circulates through the undecaying branches. "Unless the Lord build the House, they labour in vain that build it". Idle is our labour, worthless is our toil, ashes is our fruit, corruption is our reward, unless we begin the foundation of this great undertaking in faith and prayer, and sanctify it by purity of life.

SERMON V.

DISPOSITIONS FOR FAITH.

Evang. sec. Luc., *c.* iii. *v.* 4–6.

Parate viam Domini: rectas facite semitas ejus: omnis vallis implebitur, et omnis mons et collis humiliabitur: et erunt prava in directa, et aspera in vias planas: et videbit omnis caro salutare Dei.

Prepare ye the way of the Lord, make straight His path. Every valley shall be filled, and every mountain and hill shall be brought low; and the crooked shall be made straight, and the rough ways plain: and all flesh shall see the salvation of God.

THE Holy Baptist was sent before our Lord to prepare His way; that is, to be His instrument in rousing, warning, humbling, and inflaming the hearts of men, so that, when He came, they might believe in Him. He Himself is the Author and Finisher of that Faith, of which He is also the Object; but, ordinarily, He does not implant it in us suddenly, but He first creates certain dispositions, and these He carries on to faith as their reward. When then He was about to appear on earth among His chosen people, and to claim for Himself their faith, He made use of St. John first to create in them these necessary dispositions; and therefore it is that, at this season, when we are about to celebrate His birth, we commemorate again and again the great Saint who was His forerunner, as in to-day's Gospel, lest we should forget, that, without a due preparation of heart, we cannot hope to obtain and keep the all-important gift of faith.

It is observable too, that, on this same day, just the fifth day before Christmas, we are accustomed to celebrate the feast of St. Thomas, who for a while incurred the sin of unbelief; as if our tender Mother, Holy Church, as an additional safeguard, would make an example of the great Apostle for our sakes, and held him up to us, who now reigns with Christ in heaven, in the image of his earthly weakness, in order to force us to consider that certain dispositions of mind are necessary for faith, and how the want of them shows itself, and wherein lies its fault.

I think, then, that I shall be taking a subject suitable both to the season and the day, if I attempt to set before you, my Brethren, as far as time permits, how it is, humanly speaking, that a man comes to believe the revealed word of God, and why one man believes and another does not. And, in describing the state of mind and of thought which leads to faith, I shall not of course be forgetting that faith, as I have already said, is a supernatural work, and the fruit of divine grace; I only shall be calling your attention to what must be your own part in the process.

As to the account, given us in Scripture, of St. Thomas's incredulity, its prominent points are these:—first, that, when told by his brethren that our Lord was risen, he said, "Except I shall see in His hands the print of the nails, and put my finger into the place of the nails, and put my hand into His side, I will not believe". Now, here the question is, What was wrong in this? for the other Apostles *had* seen and touched our Lord, and appear not to have believed till they did. Secondly, that our Lord said to him on a subsequent occasion, after allowing to him the evidence he desired, "Because thou hast seen Me, Thomas, thou hast believed; blessed are they that have not seen, and have believed". Now, *why* is it blessed to believe in Him without seeing, rather than to have that sight of Him which other Apostles had when they believed?

The subject is a very large one: I shall attempt to follow out only one out of various trains of thought to which it gives rise.

Now, first, I think it will be granted by any one who knows Scripture well, that the doctrine laid down by our Lord on the occasion in question, He had expressed on other occasions and in other ways. For instance, He said, "Unless you see signs and wonders, you believe not". Elsewhere we read, "He wrought not many miracles then, because of their unbelief". In these passages He implies that hardness of belief is a fault. Elsewhere He praises easiness of belief. For instance, "O woman, great is thy faith". "Amen, I say to you, I have not found so great faith in Israel". "Be of good heart, daughter, thy faith hath made thee whole". "Thy faith hath made thee safe, go in peace". "If thou canst believe, all things are possible to him that believeth". I might quote many other passages to the same effect, from the Gospels, the Acts of the Apostles, and St. Paul's Epistles.

Now these passages cannot mean that faith is against reason, or that reason does not ordinarily precede faith, for this is a doctrine quite contrary to Revelation, but I think I shall not be wrong in understanding them thus,—that with good dispositions faith *is* easy, and that without good dispositions, faith is *not* easy; and that those who were praised for their faith, were such as had already the good dispositions, and that those who were blamed for their unbelief, were such as were wanting in this respect, and would have believed, or believed sooner, had they possessed the necessary dispositions for believing, or a greater share of them. This is the point I am going to insist on: I am led to it by the Baptist's especial office of "preparing the way of the Lord"; for by that preparation is meant the creating in the hearts of his hearers the dispositions necessary for faith. And I consider that the same truth is implied in the glorious hymn of the Angels upon Christmas night; for to whom was the Prince of Peace to come? They sang, "Glory to God in the highest, and on earth *peace to men of good will*". By "good will" is meant, " good disposition"; the peace of the Gospel, the full gifts of the knowledge, and of the power, and of the consolation of Christian Redemption, were to be the reward of men of *good dispositions*. *They* were the men to whom the Infant Saviour came; *they* were those in whom His grace would find its fruit and recompense; *they* were those, who, by congruous merit, would be led on, as the Evangelist says, to " *believe* in His Name", and " to be born, not of blood, nor of the will of the flesh, nor of the will of man, but of God".

Now, in order to show what this good will, or good disposition, is, and how it bears upon faith, I observe as follows: What is the main guide of the soul, given to the whole race of Adam, outside the true fold of Christ as well as within it, given from the first dawn of reason, given to it in spite of that grievous penalty of ignorance, which is one of the chief miseries of our fallen state? It is the light of conscience, "the True Light", as the same Evangelist says, in the same passage, "which enlighteneth every man that cometh into this world". Whether a man be born in pagan darkness, or in some corruption of revealed religion,—whether he has heard the Name of the Saviour of the world or not,— whether he be the slave of some superstition,— or is in possession of some portions of Scripture, and treats the inspired word as a sort of philosophical book, which he interprets for himself, and comes to certain conclusions about its teaching,—in any case, he has within his breast a certain commanding dictate, not a mere sentiment, not a mere opinion, or impression, or view of things, but a law, an authoritative voice, bidding him do certain things and avoid others. I do not say that its particular injunctions are always clear, or that they are always consistent with each other; but what I am insisting on here is this, that it *commands*,—that it praises, it blames, it promises, it threatens, it implies a future, and it witnesses of the unseen. It is more than a man's own self. The man himself has not power over it, or only with extreme difficulty; he did not make it, he cannot destroy it. He may silence it in particular cases or directions, he may distort its enunciations, but he cannot, or it is quite the exception if he can, he cannot emancipate himself from it. He can disobey it, he may refuse to use it; but it remains.

This is Conscience; and, from the nature of the case, its very existence carries on our minds to a Being exterior to ourselves; for else whence did it come? and to a being superior to ourselves; else whence its strange, troublesome peremptoriness? I say, without going on to the question *what* it says, and whether its particular dictates are always as clear and consistent as they might be, its very existence throws us out of ourselves, and beyond ourselves, to go and seek for Him in the height and depth, whose Voice it is. As the sunshine implies that the sun is in the heavens, though we may see it not, as a knocking at our doors at night implies the presence of one outside in the dark who asks for admittance, so this Word within us, not only instructs us up to a certain point, but necessarily raises our minds to the idea of a Teacher, an unseen Teacher: and in proportion as we listen to that Word, and use it, not only do we learn more from it, not only do its dictates become clearer and its lessons broader and its principles more consistent, but its very tone is louder and more authoritative and constraining. And thus it is, that to those who use what they have, more is given; for, beginning with obedience, they go on to the intimate perception and belief of one God. His Voice within them witnesses to Him, and they believe His own witness about Himself. They believe in His existence, not because others say it, not on the word of man merely, but with a personal apprehension of its truth. This, then, is the first step in those good dispositions which lead to faith in the Gospel.

And my second remark is this: that, in spite of all that this Voice does for them, it does not do enough, as they most keenly and sorrowfully feel. They find it most difficult to separate what it really says, taken by itself, from what their own passion or pride, self-love or self-will, mingles with it. Many is the time when they cannot tell how much that true inward Guide commands, and how much comes from a mere earthly source. So that the gift of conscience raises a desire for what it does not itself fully supply. It inspires in them the idea of authoritative guidance, of a divine law; and the desire of possessing it in its fulness, not in mere fragmentary portions or indirect suggestions. It creates in them a thirst, an impatience, for the knowledge of that Unseen Lord, and Governor, and Judge, who as yet speaks to them only secretly, who whispers in their hearts, who tells them something, but not nearly so much as they wish and as they need. Thus you see, my Brethren, a religious man, who has not the blessing of the infallible teaching of revelation, is led to *look out* for it, for the very reason that he *is* religious. He has something, but not all; and if he did not desire more, it would be a proof that he had not used, that he had not profited by, what he had. Hence he will be on the look-out. Such is the definition, I may say, of every religious man, who has not the knowledge of Christ: he is on the look-out. As the Jewish believers were on the look-out for a Messias whom they knew was to come, so at all times, and under all dispensations, and in all sects, there are those who know there is a truth, who know they do not possess it except in a very low measure, who desire to know more, who know that He alone who has taught them what they know, can teach them more, who hope that He *will* teach them more, and so are on the look-out for His teaching.

There is another reason why they will be thus waiting and watching for some further knowledge of God's will than they at present possess. It is because the more a person tries to obey his conscience, the more he gets alarmed at himself, for obeying it so imperfectly. His sense of duty will become more keen, and his perception of transgression more delicate, and he will understand more and more how many things he has to be forgiven. But next, while he thus grows in self-knowledge, he also understands more and more clearly that the voice of conscience has nothing gentle, nothing of mercy in its tone. It is severe and even stern. It does not speak of forgiveness, but of punishment. It suggests to him a future judgment; it does not tell him how he can avoid it. Moreover, it does not tell him how he is to get better; he feels himself very sinful at the best; he feels himself in bondage to a tyranny which, alas! he loves too well, even while he hates it. And thus he is in great anguish, and cries out in the Apostle's words, "Unhappy man that I am, who shall deliver me from the body of this death?"

For all these reasons then,—because he feels his ignorance, because he feels his bondage, because he feels his guilt and danger,—a religious man who has not the blessing of revelation, will be on the look-out for revelation. And this is the second disposition leading to faith in Christ:

the first was belief in God, as our Teacher, Governor, and Judge; and the second is the earnest desire that He would reveal Himself, and an eager looking-out for the chance of His doing so.

This is the state of mind of the elect few: now, on the other hand, let us consider the state of mind of the multitude, who think little or nothing of religion, who disobey their conscience. who think as little of its dictates as they can, who would get rid of it, if they could. What will *they* know of the convictions, the apprehensions, and the hopes and wishes, of which I have been speaking? Will they have any nervous anxiety, any painful longing to be brought out of their present darkness? Will they, being, as I am supposing, strangers to revealed truth, will they be on the look-out for revelation? What is revelation to them? What do they care how sins are to be forgiven, when they do not feel the burden of sin? What desire have they for strength greater than their own to overcome their passions or their pride, seeing that they make much of their pride, as their true dignity, and freely indulge their passions, as their sole joy? They are contented with themselves; they

DISPOSITIONS FOR FAITH. 91

think themselves as happily conditioned as they can be under the circumstances; they only wish to be let alone; they have no need of priest or prophet; they live in their own way and in their own home, pursuing their own tastes, never looking out of doors; perhaps with natural virtues, perhaps not, but with no distinct or consistent religious sense. Thus they live, and thus they die. Such is the character of the many, all over the earth; they live, to all appearance, in some object of this world, and never rise above the world, and, it is plain, have nothing of those dispositions at all, which lead to faith.

Now take a man from each of these two classes, and suppose the news actually reaches them both, that a message has been received from the unseen world: how will they respectively act? It is plain: on him who has been looking out, or hoping, or at least longing, for such a mercy, its operation will be wonderful. It will affect him profoundly; it will thrill through him; so much so, that, provided only the message, on examination, be of a nature to answer his needs, he will be under a strong temptation to believe it, if he can, on very little evidence, or on none at all. At all events he will set about inquiring what its evidence is, and will do his best to find it all out, whether it be more or less. On the other hand, the man, who is without the due religious dispositions I have been describing, simply is not moved at all. He takes no interest in the report, and will not go to the pains to inquire about it. He will sit at home; and it will not even occur to him that he ought to rise, and look about him. He is as little stirred, as if he heard that a great man had arisen in the antipodes, or that there was a revolution in Japan. Here then we have come to the critical difference between the two descriptions of men. The one is active, and the other passive, when Christ is preached as the Saviour of the world. The one goes to meet the Truth; the other thinks that the Truth ought to come to *him*. The one examines into the proof that God has spoken; the other waits till this is proved to him. He feels no personal interest in it; he thinks it not his own concern, but (if I may so say) God Almighty's concern. He does not care to make the most of his knowledge; he does not put things together; he does not add up his facts and cumulate his arguments; he leaves all this to be done for him by Him who speaks to him; and if he is to have any trouble in the matter, then he is willing to dismiss it altogether. And next, supposing proof is actually offered him, he feels no sort of gratitude or delicacy towards Him who offers it: he says without compunction, "I do not see this"; and "that does not follow"; for he is a critic and a judge, not an inquirer, and he negociates and bargains, when he ought to be praying for light. And thus he learns nothing rightly, and goes the way to reject a divine message, because he will not throw himself upon and into the evidence; while his neighbour, who has a real concern for his own salvation, finds it and believes.

Returning, then, to what I said when I began, we see now how it was that our Lord praised easiness of belief, and condemned hardness of belief. To be easy in believing is nothing more or less than to have been ready to inquire; to be hard of belief is nothing else but to have been loth and reluctant to inquire. Those whose faith He praised had no stronger evidence than those whose unbelief He condemned; but they had used their eyes, used their reason, exerted their minds, and persevered in inquiry till they found; while the others, whose unbelief He condemned, had heard indeed, but had let the divine seed lie by the roadside, or in the rocky soil, or among the thorns which choked it. And here I am led to say, what seems to me, as far as it is reverent to conjecture it, the fault of the holy Apostle St. Thomas. He said that he would not believe that our Lord had risen, unless he actually saw Him. What! is there not more than one way of arriving at faith in Christ? are there not a hundred proofs, distinct from each other, and all good ones? Was there no way of being sure He came from God, except that of seeing the great miracle of the resurrection? Surely there were many others; but St. Thomas prescribed the only mode in which he would consent to believe in Him. This was the case of his countrymen also, for in this point he only did what they had done. The Jews had long been the people of God, and they had the writings of the Prophets. The fulfilment of the Prophecies in the Person of our Lord was the most obvious and natural evidence to the Jews that He was the Messias; but they would not accept this evidence, and determined to have another. They determined to be convinced in one particular way, viz., by miracles; and when, out of the superabundant mercy of God, miracles were wrought before their eyes, then they would choose the special kind of miracle which was to convince them, and would not believe, unless it was a miracle to their liking. And hence it was that our Lord said, as I have already quoted His words: "Unless ye see signs and wonders, ye believe not". Hence too He said, on other occasions: "O foolish and slow of heart to believe in all things which the *Prophets* have spoken". And: "If they hear not Moses and the *Prophets*, neither will they believe if one rise again from the dead". And: "An evil and adulterous generation seeketh a sign, and a sign shall not be given it, but the sign of Jonas the *Prophet*". And hence the Jews of Thessalonica are censured, and the Bereans, on the contrary, praised, "who received the word with all eagerness, daily *searching the Scriptures*, whether these things were so". It is added, "and many of them *believed*". And therefore, in the instance of St. Thomas, I say that, when he was so slow to believe, his fault lay in thinking he had a right to be fastidious, and to pick and choose by what arguments he would be convinced, instead of asking himself whether he had not enough to convince him already; just as if, forsooth, it were a great matter to his Lord that he should believe, and no matter at all to himself. And therefore it was, that, while Christ so graciously granted him the kind of proof he desired, He said to him for our sakes: "Because thou hast seen Me, Thomas, thou hast believed: blessed are they that have not seen, and have believed".

And so, alas! it is now: many is the man who has a drawing towards the Catholic Church, and resists it, on the plea that he has not sufficient proof of her claims. Now he cannot have proof all at once, he cannot be converted all at once, I grant; but he *can* inquire; he can determine to resolve the doubt, before he puts it aside, though it cost labour and time to do so. The intimate feeling of his heart should be: "What must I do, that I may be saved?" His best consolation, the promise: "Ask, and it shall be given you; seek, and you shall find; knock, and it shall be opened to you". If, instead of this, he quarrels with this or that particular proof, never thinks of inquiring for himself, and ascertaining where the truth lies, contents himself with admiring the Church, and so ends the matter, what is this but the conduct of one who has no sensitive conscience, who loves his own ease, or the comforts of life, or his worldly reputation, or the society of his relatives, or his worldly interests, and considers that religious truth is not worth the sacrifice of these temporal advantages?

Do not fancy, my Brethren, that what I have been saying about inquirers, in no sense applies to you. Catholics, indeed, have not to seek; the anxious questions which natural conscience asks, are in your case answered to the full. You know who saves you, and how; but recollect that that same sensitiveness and delicacy of conscience, which is the due disposition for faith, is also its safeguard and its nutriment, when it is at length possessed. It feeds the flame of faith, and makes it burn brightly. St. Paul speaks of those, who, having "rejected a good conscience", had "made shipwreck of their faith". This will be particularly the case in a day like this. Catholics go into the world; they mix with men of all religions; they hear all manner of sophistical objections made to the Church, her doctrines, and her rules. What is practically to keep them steadfast in the faith, but their intimate perception of their need of it? what is to bring them to the sacrament of penance, but their sorrow and their detestation of sin? what is to bring them to communion, but a thirst for the Living and True God? what is to be their protection against the aberrations of the intellect, but the deep convictions and eager aspirations of the heart?

My dear Brethren, this is a day in which much stress is laid upon the *arguments* producible for believing Religion, Natural and Revealed; and books are written to prove that we ought to believe, and why. These books are called Natural Theology and Evidences of Christianity; and it is often said by our enemies, that Catholics do not know why they believe. Now I have no intention whatever of denying the beauty and the cogency of the arguments which these books contain; but I question much, whether in matter of fact they make or keep men Christians. I have no such doubt about the argument which I have been here recommending to you. Be sure, my Brethren, that the best argument, better than all the books in the world, better than all that astronomy, and geology, and physiology, and all other sciences, can supply,— an argument intelligible to those who cannot read as well as to those who can,— an argument which is "within us",—an argument intellectually conclusive, and practically persuasive, whether for proving the Being of a God, or for laying the ground for Christianity,—is that which arises out of a careful attention to the teachings of our heart, and a comparison between the claims of conscience and the announcements of the Gospel.

SERMON VI.

OMNIPOTENCE IN BONDS.

Evang. sec. Luc., *c.* ii. *v.* 51.

Et descendit cum eis, et venit Nazareth: et erat subditus illis.

And He went down with them, and came to Nazareth; and was subject to them.

AT this Christmas season, when we are celebrating those joyful mysteries, which ushered in the Gospel, it seems almost an officious intrusion upon our holiday to engage in any exercise of the reason, even though it be in order to enliven the devotional feelings proper to the holy tide. It is a time of religious rest and spiritual festivity, and even on the ground that discussion is a kind of labour, we seem to have a right to be protected against it. And yet, as the days go on, and thankfulness has had free current and joy has had its fill, it seems allowable too, to look back at length on what has been occupying the heart, and

OMNIPOTENCE IN BONDS. 101

to reason upon it. Nay, we seem to have the highest of possible authorities for doing so; for after two of the joyful mysteries, the third and the fifth, the holy Virgin is said to have done this very thing. Upon the Nativity of our Lord and Saviour, the very feast we have been celebrating, the Evangelist tells us, " Mary kept all these words, *pondering* them in her heart"; and after she had found Him in the Temple in the midst of the Doctors, which is the subject of this day's Gospel, "His Mother", we are told, "kept all these words in her heart". Surely, then, it is permitted to me, consistently with the love and adoration due to this happy time of Christmas, to direct your minds, my Brethren, to a consideration which it suggests, not indeed very recondite, on the contrary, obvious to all of us, lying on the very face of the great Mystery, but calculated, I think, both to strengthen the faith and to deepen the love, with which we receive it into our hearts.

" The Word was made flesh, and dwelt among us"; this is the glorious, unsearchable, incomprehensible Truth, on which all our hopes for the future depend, and which we have now been commemorating. It is the wonderful Economy of Redemption, by which God became man, the Highest became the lowest, the Creator took His place among His own creatures, Power became weakness, and Wisdom looked to men like folly. He that was rich was made poor; the Lord of all was rejected: "He came unto His own, and His own received Him not". This, I say, is the grand mystery of the season, and this is the subject on which I now propose to make one remark.

I say then, my Brethren, consider what the Divine Being is, and what we mean when we use His name. The very first idea of Him, if we make the Creed our guide, is Omnipotence: "I believe in God, the Father Almighty". And if you wish to enter into this idea of Omnipotence, and investigate what it is, trace it back into the further mystery of a past eternity. For ages innumerable, for infinite periods, long and long before any creature existed, He was. When there was no creature to exercise His power upon, still He was Omnipotent in His very Essence, as being not sovereign merely, but sole,—as the One Being, without any greater, less, or equal, full of all resources within, and in need of nothing, and, though infinitely one, yet being, at the same time, a whole infinite universe, as I may say, in Himself;—so much so that the breadth and depth and richness and variety and splendour of this created world which we behold, is simply nothing at all, compared to the vastness of that Ocean of perfection which lay concentrated in the intensity of His unity. A king of this world, though a sovereign, though an autocrat, depends on his subjects; but the Almighty God is absolutely and utterly free from any necessary alliance with His creatures. He is complete in Himself, for this reason, if for no other, that He existed for everlasting ages before any one of them was, and was able to do without them for a past eternity, and then created them all out of nothing. He borrows nothing from them; He owes nothing whatever even to the highest of them; they, on the contrary, owe it to Him that they are even able to remain in their own proper nature, and they derive from Him, moment by moment, every pulsation of their life and every ray of such glory as they possess.

Such is the omnipotent, self-dependent God: fixed in His own centre, and needing no point of motion or vantage-ground out of Himself, whereupon to bring into action, or to use, or to apply, His inexhaustible power. He can make, He can unmake; He can decree and bring to pass, He can direct, control, and resolve, absolutely according to His will. He could create this vast material world, with all its suns and globes and its illimitable spaces, in a moment. All its overwhelming multiplicity of laws, and complexity of formations, and intricacy of contrivances, both to originate and to accomplish, is with Him but the work of a moment. He could destroy it all in all its parts in a moment; in the same one moment He could create another universe instead of it, indefinitely more vast, more beautiful, more marvellous, and indefinitely unlike that universe which He was annihilating. He could bring into existence and destroy an infinite series of such universes, each in succession more perfect than that which immediately preceded it. He is the Creator, too, of all the intellectual natures which exist, whether in the heavens above, or on the earth, or in the regions under the earth. Angels in their nine multitudinous orders, and men in their populous generations, good spirits and bad, saints and souls on trial, the saved and the lost, first, He created them and creates, each in its own time; and next, He keeps the complete and exact tale of them all, as He keeps the catalogue also of all the beasts, the birds, the fishes, the reptiles, and insects, all over the earth. Not a sparrow falls without Him; not a hair of our heads, but He has counted it in with the rest; and so, too, not a soul, but He has before Him its whole history from beginning to end, and its every thought, word, and deed, and its every motion through every day, and its relative place in the scale of merit and of sin.

And, while He thus intermingles His presence and His operations with an ineffable intimacy of union in every place, in every substance, in every act, every where, He is at the same time, as I have said, infinitely separated from everything, and absolutely incommunicable and unapproachable and self-dependent in his own glorious Essence. Nothing can add to Him; no one can be His creditor, no one can claim anything of Him. He has no duties (if I may use such a term) towards the beings He has created. It is a saying about earthly possessions, that property has its duties as well as its privileges. Such words and such ideas apply not to the Self-subsisting, Everlasting God. He asks of His creatures, "Is it not lawful for Me to do what I will?" And St. Paul says of Him: "O man! who art thou that repliest against God? shall the thing formed, say to Him who formed it, Why hast Thou made me thus?" If I must still use the word "duties" or obligations of Almighty God, I will say, that He has obligations towards Himself, but none towards us. What binds Him is the dictate of His own holy and perfect attributes. He is just and true, because His attributes are such; but we have no claims upon Him. Or, if we have claims, it is in consequence of His own gratuitous and express promise, by which indeed He does bind Himself; and then He is but faithful to His own word, because He is the Truth, and His obligation is to Himself, and not to us. You know, my Brethren, we, in our turn, have no duties towards the brute creation; there is no relation of justice between them and us. Of course we are bound not to treat them ill, for cruelty is an offence against that holy Law which our Maker has written on our hearts, and is displeasing to Him. But *they* can claim nothing at our hands; into our hands they are absolutely delivered. We may use them, we may destroy them at our pleasure, not our wanton pleasure, but still for our own ends, for our own benefit or satisfaction, provided we can give a rational account of what we do. Now, I do not say that the case is the same between us and our Maker, but it is illustrated by this parallel. He has no account at all to render to us: He has no claims of ours to settle: we are bound to Him; He is not bound to us, except as He binds Himself: we have no merit in His sight, and can do Him no service, unless His promise brings these ideas into existence. I say, He is only bound by His own perfect Nature, infinitely good, and holy, and true, as It is; and in that is the creature's stay. If we accuse Him, He will prevail, according to the text, "that Thou mayest be justified in thy words, and mayest overcome when Thou art judged". And if we are utterly without claims upon Him as creatures, we are doubly destitute considered as sinners also: and thus, if even Angels are unprofitable in His sight, what are we?

In the words of Holy Scripture:* " Can a man be compared with God? What doth it profit God, if thou be just? or what dost thou give Him, if thy way be unspotted? Behold, even

---

* *Job*, iv., ix., xv., xxii., xxv., xxxiii.

the moon doth not shine, and the stars are not pure in His sight. Behold, among His saints, none is unchangeable, and the heavens are not pure in His sight. Behold, they that serve Him are not steadfast, and in His Angels He found wickedness. How much more is man abominable and unprofitable, who drinketh iniquity like water! Behold, He taketh away, and who can hinder Him? Who will say to Him: What dost Thou? Why dost thou strive against Him? for He giveth not account of any of His matters".

Such is the Omnipotence, the Self-dependence, the Self-sufficiency, the infinite Liberty of the Eternal God, our Creator and Judge. And now, this being so, let me go on to the particular thought which I wish, my Brethren, to suggest to you for your reflection at this season.

It is, not merely that God became man, not merely that the All-possessing became destitute; but the point on which I shall particularly insist is, in contrast with what I have been enlarging on, that the All-powerful, the All-free, the Infinite, became and becomes, as the text says, "subject" to the creature; nay, not only a subject, but literally a captive, a prisoner, and that not once, but on many different occasions and in many different ways.

Now, observe, my Brethren, when the Eternal Son of God came among us, He might have taken our nature, as Adam received it, from the earth, and have begun His human life at mature age; He might have been moulded under the immediate hand of the Creator; He need have known nothing of the feebleness of infancy or the slow growth of manhood. This might have been, had He so willed; but no: He preferred the penance of taking His place in the line of Adam, and of being born of a woman. This was the very scandal of the ancient heretics, as it has been of free-thinkers in all ages. They shrank from the notion of such a birth from Mary, as a something simply intolerable and past belief; and truly in that belief is the commencement of the wonderful captivity of the Infinite God, on which I am to dwell. Yet I will not do more than suggest so much of it to your devout meditation. I mean the long imprisonment He had, before His birth, in the womb of the Immaculate Mary. There was He in His human nature, who, as God, is every where; there was

He, as regards His human soul, conscious from the first with a full intelligence, and feeling the extreme irksomeness of the prison-house, full of grace as it was.

At length He sees the light, and He is free; but free only in that His imprisonment is changed. The very first act of His Mother's on His birth, is both an example and a figure of His life-long captivity. "Mary brought forth her first-born Son, and wrapped Him up in swaddling clothes, and laid Him in a manger". It is the custom in those southern parts to treat the new-born babe in a way strange to this age and country. The infant is swathed around with cloths much resembling the winding-sheet, the bandages and ligaments of the dead. You may recollect, my Brethren, the account of Lazarus's revival; how that, when miracle had lifted him up out of the tomb, there he lay motionless, till his fastenings were cut off from him. "He that had been dead came forth, bound foot and hand with winding-bands; and Jesus said to them: Loose him, and let him go". So was it with that wonder-working Lord Himself in His own infancy. He submitted to the customs, as well as to the ritual, of His nation; and, as He had lain so long in Mary's womb, so now again He left that sacred prison, only that her loving hands might manacle and fetter Him once more, inflicting on Him the special penance which He had chosen. And so, like some inanimate image of wood or stone, the All-powerful lies in the manger, or on her bosom, doubly helpless, both because His infancy is feeble, and because His bonds are strong.

It is in this wise He was shown to the shepherds; thus He was worshipped by the wise men; thus He was presented in the Temple, taken up in Simeon's arms, hurried off to Egypt by night, His tender Mother adoring the while that abject captivity to which it was her awful duty to reduce Him. So His first months passed; and, though as time went on, He grew in stature, and burst His bonds, still through a slow and tedious advance did He enter on His adolescence. And then, when for a moment He anticipated His mission, and sat down among the Doctors in the Temple, He was quickly recalled by His Mother's chiding, and went back again to her and Joseph, and in the emphatic words of the text, was " subject unto them". It is said, He worked at His father's trade, not even yet His own master, and confined till the age of thirty to the limits of one city.

And when at length the hour came for His breaking away from his humble home and quitting Nazareth, even then this law of captivity, as I may call it, continued, and that even with the circumstances of a frightful development. For is it not terrifying, so as even to scare the mind, that in His infancy indeed His Mother's pure embrace had been His prison, but now, as a preparation for His public ministry, He is made over to His enemy, and undergoes the handling of the foul spirit himself! The rebel archangel, who would *not* be in subjection, who had assailed the throne of God, and had been cast out of heaven, he it is, who now has got fast hold of the Eternal Word Incarnate, and is lifting Him up, and transporting Him according to his will; taking Him into the holy city, and setting Him upon the pinnacle of the Temple, and taking Him up into a very high mountain, in order to seduce Him with the bribe of the unshackled lordship of the wide earth. "What concord hath Christ with Belial?" Yet the fiend is allowed the momentary possession of the Omnipotent.

But at least when He has begun to preach, He

will be free. My Brethren, it is true; but even then the threatenings at least and the earnests of a renewed captivity pursue Him. As soon as He does miracles and collects followers, His brethren take the alarm, and try to capture Him. "When His friends had heard of it, they went out to lay hold of Him, for they said, He is become mad". When He preached in Nazareth, "the people rose and seized Him violently, and brought Him to the brow of the hill, to cast Him headlong". At another time He was in danger from His own hearers; they went about to take Him by force to make Him a king. At another time, "the Scribes and Pharisees sent ministers to apprehend Him". At another time, Herod was about to seize Him and put Him to death.

At length He is to die for us; but still that sacrifice was not to please Him, if imprisonment was away. He allowed Himself, in the words of the Church, "manibus tradi nocentium", to be given into the hands of the violent. Now, I ask, what need of this superfluity of humiliation? He was to shed His blood and die; doubtless: but in the manifold dispositions of Providence there were many ways whereby to die, without falling into the fierce handling of jailers and hangmen.

He might have taken upon Himself the mode of satisfying the Divine Decree, and have dispensed with the instrumentality of man. We read in history of kings going to death, who refused the assistance of the executioner, and submitted to their fate by their own act. And it was in order to remind us that He *need* not have undergone that profanation, that, on His enemies first approaching Him, He smote them to the ground. And again, it was in order to impress upon us that He *did* undergo it, that He touchingly asked them: "Are ye come out as to a robber, with swords and clubs, to apprehend Me? but this is your hour and the power of darkness".

Thus He spoke, and that expostulation was the immediate signal for those special indignities to begin in which He chose to invest His passion and death. He who was submitted to the winepress in Gethsemani, and agonized with none to see Him but Apostles and attendant Angels, might surely have gone through His solemn sacrifice in solitude, as He commenced it; but He preferred the "hands of men"; He preferred the loathsome kiss of the traitor; He preferred the staves and swords of the ministers of a fallen priesthood; He preferred to die in the midst of a

furious mob, haling Him to and fro; under the
fists and scourges and hammers of savage lictors;
now shut up in a dungeon, now dragged before
the judgment-seat, now tied to a pillar, now
nailed to the Cross, and then at length, when the
worst was over, and His soul was fled, hurried
as the best His friends could do for Him, hurried
into a narrow sepulchre of stone. O marvellous
dispensation, full of mystery! that the God of Nature, the Lord of the Universe, should take to
Himself a body to suffer and die in; nor only so,
but should not even allow Himself the birthright
of man, should refuse to be master of His own
limbs, and outgrow the necessity of a Mother's
arms, only to present Himself to the tyrannous
grasp of the heathen soldiers.

And now surely, my Brethren, we are come
to the end of these wonders. He tore open the
solid rock; He rose from the tomb; He ascended
on high; He is far off from the earth; He is safe
from profanation; and the soul and body, which
He assumed, partake of course, as far as created
nature allows, of the Sovereign Freedom and
the Independence of Omnipotence. It is not so:
He is indeed beyond the reach of suffering; but
you anticipate, my Brethren, what I have yet to

say. Is He then so enamoured of the prison, that He should purpose to revisit earth again, in order that, as far as possible, He may undergo it still? Does He set such a value on subjection to His creatures, that, before He goes away, on the very eve of His betrayal, He must actually make provision, after death, for perpetuating His captivity to the end of the world? My Brethren, the great truth is daily before our eyes: He has ordained the standing miracle of His Body under visible symbols, that He may secure thereby the standing mystery of Omnipotence in bonds.

He took bread, and blessed, and made it His Body; He took wine, and gave thanks, and made it His Blood; and He gave His priests the power to do what He had done. Henceforth, He is in the hands of sinners once more. Frail, ignorant, sinful man, by the sacerdotal power given to him, compels the presence of the Highest; he lays Him up in a small tabernacle; he dispenses Him to a sinful people. Those who are only just now cleansed from mortal sin, open their lips for Him; those who are soon to return to mortal sin, receive Him into their breasts; those who are polluted with vanity and selfishness and ambition and pride, presume to make Him their guest; the frivolous, the tepid, the worldly-minded, fear not to welcome Him. Alas! alas! even those who wish to be more in earnest, entertain Him with cold and wandering thoughts, and quench that Love which would inflame them with Its own fire, did they but open to It. Such are the best of us; and then for the worst! O my Brethren, what shall we say of sacrilege? of His reception into hearts polluted with mortal, unforsaken sin? of those further nameless profanations, which from time to time occur, when unbelief dares to present itself at the Holy Altar, and blasphemously gains possession of Him?

My Brethren, it is plain that, when we confess God as Omnipotent only, we have gained but a half-knowledge of Him: His is an Omnipotence which can at the same time swathe Itself in infirmity and can become the captive of Its own creatures. He has, if I may so speak, the incomprehensible power of even making Himself weak. We must know Him by His Names, Emmanuel and Jesus, to know Him perfectly.

One word more before I conclude. Some persons may consider that a thought, such as that I have been enlarging on, is a difficulty to

faith. Every one has his own trials and his own
scandals: I grant it. For me, my Brethren, I can
only say that its effect on myself lies just in the
very opposite direction, and, awful as it is, it
does but suggest matter, as for adoration, so for
faith also. What human teacher could thus
open for us an insight into the infinitude of the
Divine Counsels? Eye of man hath not seen
the face of God; and heart of man could never
have conceived or invented so wonderful a manifestation, as the Gospel contains, of His ineffable,
overwhelming Attributes. I believe the infinite
condescension of the Highest to be true, because
it has been imagined. Moreover, I recognize it
to be true, just as I believe in the laws of this
material world, according as human science elicits them; viz., because I see here the silent
operation, beneath the surface, of a great principle, which is not seen till it is investigated. I
adore a truth, which, though patent to all who
look for it, yet, to be seen in its consistency and
symmetry, has to be looked for. And further, I
glory in it, for I see in it the most awful antagonism to the very idea and essence of sin, whether as existing in Angels or in men. For what
was the sin of Lucifer, but the resolve to be his

own master? What was the sin of Adam, but impatience of subjection, and a desire to be his own god? What is the sin of all his children, but the movement, not of passion merely, not of selfishness, not of unbelief, but of pride, of the heart rising against the law of God, and set on being emancipated from its trammels? What is the sin of Antichrist, but, as St. Paul says, that of being " the Lawless One", of " opposing or being lifted up against all that is called God, or worshipped, so that he sitteth in the temple of God, showing himself as if he were God"? If, then, the very principle of sin is insubordination, is there not a stupendous meaning in the fact, that He, the Eternal, who alone is sovereign and supreme, has given us an example in His own Person of that love of subjection, which in Him alone is simply voluntary, but in all creatures is an elementary duty?

O my Brethren, let us blush at our own pride and self-will. Let us call to mind our impatience at God's providences towards us, our wayward longings after what cannot be, our headstrong efforts to reverse His just decrees, our bootless conflicts with the stern necessities which hem us in, our irritation at ignorance or suspense about His will, our fierce, passionate wilfulness when we see that will too clearly, our haughty contempt of His ordinances, our determination to do things for ourselves without Him, our preference of our own reason to His word,— the many, many shapes in which the Old Adam shows itself, and one or other of which our conscience tells us is our own; and let us pray Him who is independent of us all, yet who at this season became as though our fellow and our servant, to teach us our place in His wide universe, and to make us ambitious only of that grace here and glory hereafter, which He has purchased for us by His own humiliation.

SERMON VII.

ST. PAUL'S CHARACTERISTIC GIFT.

Ep. II. S. Paul ad Cor., c. xii. v. 9.

Libenter igitur gloriabor in infirmitatibus meis, ut inhabitet in me virtus Christi.

Gladly therefore will I glory in my infirmities, that the power of Christ may dwell in me.

ALL the Saints, from the beginning of history to the end, resemble each other in this, that their excellence is supernatural, their deeds heroic, their merits extraordinary and prevailing. They all are choice patterns of the theological virtues; they all are blessed with a rare and special union with their Maker and Lord; they all lead lives of penance; and when they leave this world, they are spared that torment, which the multitude of holy souls are allotted, between earth and heaven, death and eternal glory. But, with all these various tokens of their belonging to one and the same celestial family, they may still be divided, in their external aspect, into two classes.

There are those, on the one hand, who are so absorbed in the divine life, that they seem, even while they are in the flesh, to have no part in earth or in human nature; but to think, speak, and act under views, affections, and motives simply supernatural. If they love others, it is simply because they love God, and because man is the object either of His compassion or of His praise. If they rejoice, it is in what is unseen; if they feel interest, it is in what is unearthly; if they speak, it is almost with the voice of Angels; if they eat or drink, it is almost of Angels' food alone,—for it is recorded in their histories, that for weeks they have fed on nothing else but that Heavenly Bread which is the proper sustenance of the soul. Such we may suppose to have been St. John; such St. Mary Magdalen; such the hermits of the desert; such many of the holy Virgins whose lives belong to the science of mystical theology.

On the other hand, there are those, and of the highest order of sanctity too, as far as our eyes can see, in whom the supernatural combines with nature, instead of superseding it,—invigorating it, elevating it, ennobling it; and who are not the less men, because they are saints. They do not put away their natural endowments, but use them to the glory of the Giver; they do not act beside them, but through them; they do not eclipse them by the brightness of divine grace, but only transfigure them. They are versed in human knowledge; they are busy in human society; they understand the human heart; they can throw themselves into the minds of other men; and all this in consequence of natural gifts and secular education. While they themselves stand secure in the blessedness of purity and peace, they can follow in imagination the ten thousand aberrations of pride, passion, and remorse. The world is to them a book, to which they are drawn for its own sake, which they read fluently, which interests them naturally,— though, by the reason of the grace which dwells within them, they study it and hold converse with it for the glory of God and the salvation of souls. Thus they have the thoughts, feelings, frames of mind, attractions, sympathies, antipathies of other men, so far as these are not sinful, only they have these properties of human nature purified, sanctified, and exalted; and they are only made more eloquent, more poetical, more profound, more intellectual, by reason of their being more holy. In this latter class I may perhaps without presumption place many of the early Fathers, St. Chrysostom, St. Gregory Nazianzen, St. Athanasius, and above all, the great Saint of this day, St. Paul the Apostle.

I think it a happy circumstance that, in this Church, placed, as it is, under the patronage of the great Names of St. Peter and St. Paul, the special feast days of these two Apostles (for such we may account the 29th of June as regards St. Peter, and to-day as regards St. Paul) should, in the first year of our assembling here, each have fallen on a Sunday. And now that we have arrived, through God's protecting Providence, at the latter of these two days, the Conversion of St. Paul, I do not like to forego the opportunity, with whatever misgivings as to my ability, of offering to you, my Brethren, at least a few remarks upon the wonderful work of God's creative grace mercifully presented to our inspection in the person of this great Apostle. Most unworthy of him, I know, is the best that I can say; and even that best I cannot duly exhibit in the space of time allowed me on an occasion such as this; but what is said out of devotion to him, and for the divine glory, will, I trust, have its use, defective though it be, and be a plea for his favourable notice of those who say it, and be graciously accepted by his and our Lord and Master.

Now, since I have begun by contrasting St. Paul with St. John, and by implying that St. John lived a life more simply supernatural than St. Paul, I may seem to you, my Brethren, to be speaking to St. Paul's disparagement; and you may ask me whether it is possible for any Saint on earth whatever to have a more intimate communion with the Divine Majesty than was granted to St. Paul. You may remind me of his own words, "I live, now not I, but Christ liveth in me; and, that I now live in the flesh, I live in the faith of the Son of God, who loved me, and delivered Himself for me". And you may refer to his most astonishing ecstasies and visions; as when he was rapt even to the third heaven, and heard sacred words, which it " is not granted to man to utter". You may say, he " no way came short" of St. John in his awful initiation into the mysteries of the kingdom of heaven. Certainly you may say so; nor am I imagining anything contrary to you. We indeed cannot compare Saints; but I agree with you, that St. Paul was visited by favours, equal, in our apprehensions, to those which were granted to St. John. But then, on the other hand, neither was St. John behind St. Paul in these tokens of divine love. In truth, these tokens are some of those very things which, in a greater or less degree, belong to all Saints whatever, as I said when I began; whereas my question just now is, not what are those points in which St. Paul agrees with all other Saints, but what is his distinguished mark, how we recognize him from others, what there is special in him; and I think his characteristic is this:—that, as I have said, in him the fulness of divine gifts does not tend to destroy what is human in him, but to spiritualize and perfect it. According to his own words, used on another subject, but laying down, as it were, the principle on which his own character was formed,— "We would not be *unclothed*", he says, but " clothed *upon*, that what is mortal may be swallowed up by life". In him, his human nature, his human affections, his human gifts, were possessed and glorified by a new and heavenly life; they remained; he speaks of them in the text, and in his humility he calls them his infirmity. He was not stripped of nature, but clothed with grace and the power of Christ, and therefore he *glories* in his infirmity. This is the subject on which I wish to enlarge.

A heathen poet has said, Homo sum, humani nil mi alienum puto. "I am a man; nothing human is without interest to me": and the sentiment has been widely and deservedly praised. Now this, in a fulness of meaning which a heathen could not understand, is, I conceive, the characteristic of this great Apostle. He is ever speaking, to use his own words, " human things", and " as a man", and " according to man", and " foolishly":—that is, human nature, the common nature of the whole race of Adam, spoke in him, acted in him, with an energetical presence, with a sort of bodily fulness, always under the sovereign command of divine grace, but losing none of its real freedom and power because of its subordination. And the consequence is, that, having the nature of man so strong within him, he is able to enter into human nature, and to sympathize with it, with a gift peculiarly his own.

Now the most startling instance of this is this, —that, though his life prior to his conversion seems to have been so conscientious and so pure, nevertheless he does not hesitate to associate himself with the outcast heathen, and to speak as if he were one of them. St. Philip Neri, before he communicated, used to say, " Lord, I protest before Thee that I am good for nothing but to do evil". At confession he used to say, " I have never done one good action". He often said, " I am past hope". To a penitent he said, " Be sure of this, I am a man like my neighbours, and nothing more". Well, I mean, that somewhat in this way, St. Paul felt all his neighbours, all the whole race of Adam, to be existing in himself. He knew himself to be possessed of a nature, he was conscious of possessing a nature, which was capable of running into all the multiplicity of emotions, of devices, of purposes, and of sins, into which it had actually run in the wide world and in the multitude of men; and in that sense he bore the sins of all men, and associated himself with them, and spoke of them and himself as one. He, I say, a strict Pharisee, (as he describes himself), blameless according to legal justice, conversing with all good conscience before God, serving God from his forefathers with a pure conscience, he nevertheless elsewhere speaks of himself as a profligate heathen outcast, before the grace of God called him. He not only counts himself, as his birth made him, in the number of "children of wrath", but he classes himself with the heathen as "conversing in the desires of the flesh", "and fulfilling the will of the flesh". And in another Epistle, he speaks of himself, at the time he writes, as if "carnal, sold under sin"; he speaks of "sin dwelling in him", and of his "serving with the flesh the law of sin"; this, I say, when he was an Apostle confirmed in grace. And in like manner he speaks of concupiscence as if it were sin; all because he vividly apprehended, in that nature of his which grace had sanctified, what it was in its tendencies and results when deprived of grace.

And thus I account for St. Paul's liking for heathen writers, or what we now call the classics, which is very remarkable. He, the Apostle of the Gentiles, was learned in Greek letters, as Moses, the lawgiver of the Jews, his counterpart, was learned in the wisdom of the Egyptians; and he did not give up that learning when he had "learned Christ". I do not think I am exaggerating in saying so, since he goes out of his way three times to quote passages from them; once, speaking to the heathen Athenians; another time, to his converts at Corinth; and a third time, in a private Apostolic exhortation to his disciple St. Titus. And it is the more remarkable, that one of the writers whom he quotes seems to be a writer of comedies, which had no claim to be read for any high morality which they contain. Now how shall we account for this? Did St. Paul delight in what was licentious? God forbid:—but he had the feeling of a guardian-angel who sees every sin of the rebellious being committed to him, who gazes at him and weeps. With this difference, that he had a sympathy with sinners, which an Angel (be it reverently said) cannot have. He was a true lover of souls. He loved poor human nature with a passionate love, and the literature of the Greeks was only its expression; and he hung over it tenderly and mournfully, wishing for its regeneration and salvation.

This is how I account for his familiar knowledge of the heathen poets. Some of the ancient Fathers consider that the Greeks were under a special dispensation of Providence, preparatory to the Gospel, though not directly from heaven as the Jewish was. Now St. Paul seems, if I may say it, to partake of this feeling; distinctly as he teaches that the heathen are in darkness, and in sin, and under the power of the Evil One, he will not allow that they are beyond the eye of Divine Mercy. On the contrary, he speaks of God as "determining their times and the limits of their habitations", that is, going along with the revolutions of history and the migrations of races, "in order that they should seek Him, if haply they may feel after Him and find Him", since, he continues, "He is not far from every one of us". Again, when the Lycaonians would have worshipped him, he at once places himself on their level and reckons himself among them, and at the same time speaks of God's love of them, heathens though they were. "Ye men", he cries, "why do ye these things? We also are mortals, men like unto you"; and he adds that God in times past, though suffering all nations to walk in their own ways, nevertheless left Himself not without testimony, doing good from heaven, giving rains, and fruitful seasons, "filling our hearts with food and gladness". You see, he says, "*our* hearts", not "your", as if he were one of those Gentiles; and he dwells in a kindly human way over the food, and the gladness which food causes, which the poor heathen were granted. Hence it is that he is the Apostle who especially insists on our all coming from one father, Adam; for he had pleasure in thinking that all men were brethren. "God hath made", he says, "all mankind of one"; "as in Adam all die, so in Christ all shall be made alive". I will cite but one more passage from the great Apostle on the same subject, one in which he tenderly contemplates the captivity, and the anguish, and the longing, and the deliverance of poor human nature. "The expectation of the creature", he says, that is, of human nature, "waiteth for the manifestation of the sons of God. For the creature was made subject to vanity, not willingly, but by reason of Him that made it subject, in hope; because it shall be delivered from the servitude of corruption into the liberty of the glory of the children of God. For we know that every creature groaneth and travaileth in pain until now".

These are specimens of the tender affection which the great heart of the Apostle had for all his kind, the sons of Adam: but if he felt so much for all races spread over the earth, what did he feel for his own nation! O what a special mixture, bitter and sweet, of generous pride (if I may so speak), but of piercing, overwhelming anguish, did the thought of the race of Israel inflict upon him! the highest of nations and the lowest, his own dear people, whose glories were before his imagination and in his affection from his childhood, who had the birthright and the promise, yet who, instead of making use of them, had madly thrown them away! Alas, alas, and he himself had once been a partner in their madness, and was only saved from his infatuation by the miraculous power of God! O dearest ones, O glorious race, O miserably fallen! so high and so low! This is his tone in speaking of the Jews, at once a Jeremias and a David; David in his admiring love of them, and Jeremias in his plaintive and resigned denunciations.

Consider his words:—" I speak the truth in Christ", he says; " I lie not, my conscience bearing me witness in the Holy Ghost; that I have great sadness and continual sorrow in my heart". In spite of visions and ecstasies, in spite of his wonderful election, in spite of his manifold gifts, in spite of the cares of his Apostolate and "the solicitude for all the Churches"— you would think he had had enough otherwise both to grieve him and to gladden him,—but no, this special contemplation remains ever before his mind and in his heart. I mean, the state of his own poor people, who were in mad enmity against the promised Saviour, who had for centuries after centuries looked forward for the Hope of Israel, prepared the way for it, heralded it, suffered for it, cherished and protected it, yet, when it came, rejected it, and lost the fruit of their long patience. "Who are Israelites", he says, mournfully lingering over their past glories, "who are Israelites, to whom belongeth the adoption of children, and the glory, and the testament, and the giving of the law, and the service of God, and the promises: whose are the fathers, and of whom is Christ according to the flesh, who is over all things, God blessed for ever, Amen".

What a hard thing it was for him to give them up! He pleaded for them, while they were persecuting his Lord and himself. He reminded his Lord that he himself had also been that Lord's persecutor, and why not try them a little longer? "Lord", he said, "they know that I cast into prison, and beat in every synagogue, them that believed in Thee. And, when the blood of Stephen, Thy witness, was shed, I stood by and consented, and kept the garments of them that killed him". You see, his old frame of mind, the feelings and notions under which he persecuted his Lord, were ever distinctly before him, and he realised them as if they were still his own. "I bear them witness", he says, "that they have a zeal of God, but not according to knowledge". O blind! blind! he seems to say;—O that there should be so much of good in them, so much zeal, so much of religious purpose, so much of steadfastness, such resolve, like Josias, Mathathias, or Maccabæus, to keep the whole law, and honour Moses and the Prophets, but all spoiled, all undone, by one fatal sin! And what is he prompted to do? Moses, on one occasion, desired to suffer instead of his rebellious people: "Either forgive them this trespass", he said, "or if Thou do not, strike me out of the book". And now, when the New Law was in course of promulgation, and the chosen race was committing the same sin, its great Apostle desired the same: "I wished myself", he says, speaking of the agony he had passed through, "I wished myself to be an anathema from Christ, for my brethren, who are my kinsmen according to the flesh". And then, when all was in vain, when they remained obdurate, and the high decree of God took effect, still he would not, out of very affection for them, he would not allow after all that they were reprobate. He comforted himself with the thought of how many were the exceptions to so dismal a sentence. "Hath God cast away His people?" he asks; "God forbid. For I also am an Israelite, of the seed of Abraham, of the tribe of Benjamin". "All are not Israelites that are of Israel". And he dwells upon his confident anticipation of their recovery in time to come. "They are enemies", he says, writing to the Romans, "for your sakes"; that is, you have gained by their loss; "but they are most dear for the sake of the fathers; for the gifts and the calling of God are without repentance". "Blindness in part has happened to Israel, until the fulness of the Gentiles should come in; and so all Israel should be saved".

My Brethren, I have now explained to a certain extent what I meant when I spoke of St. Paul's characteristic gift, as being a special apprehension of human nature as a fact, and an intimate familiarity with it as an object of continual contemplation and affection. He made it his own to the very full, instead of annihilating it; he sympathized with it, while he mortified it by penance, while he sanctified it by the grace given him. Though he had never been a heathen, though he was no longer a Jew, yet he was a heathen in capability, as I may say, and a Jew in the history of the past. His vivid imagination enabled him to throw himself into the state of heathenism, with all those tendencies which lay dormant in his human nature carried out, and its infirmities developed into sin. His wakeful memory enabled him to recall those past feelings and ideas of a Jew, which in the case of others a miraculous conversion might have obliterated; and thus, while he was a Saint inferior to none, he was emphatically still a man, and to his own apprehension still a sinner.

And this being so, do you not see, my Brethren, how well fitted he was for the office of an ecumenical Doctor and an Apostle, not of the Jews only, but of the Gentiles? The Almighty sometimes works by miracle, but commonly He prepares His instruments by methods of this world; and, as He draws souls to Him, "by the cords of Adam", so does He select them for His use according to their natural powers. St. John, who lay upon His breast, whose book was the sacred heart of Jesus, and whose special philosophy was the "scientia sanctorum", *he* was not chosen to be the Doctor of the Nations. St. Peter, taught in the mysteries of the Creed, the Arbiter of doctrine and the Ruler of the faithful, he too was passed over in this work. To him specially was it given to preach to the world, who knew the world; he subdued the heart, who understood the heart. It was his sympathy that was his means of influence; it was his affectionateness which was his title and instrument of empire. "I became to the Jews a Jew", he says, "that I might gain the Jews; to them that are under the Law, as if I were under the Law, that I might gain them that were under the Law. To those that were without the Law, as if I were without the Law, that I might gain them that were without the Law. To the weak I became weak, that I might gain the weak. I became all things to all men, that I might save all".

And now, my Brethren, my time is out, before I have well begun my subject. For how can I be said yet to have entered upon the great Apostle, when I have not yet touched upon his Christian state, and his bearing towards the children of God? As yet I have chiefly spoken of his sympathy with human nature unassisted and unregenerate; not of that human life of his, when it moved and acted under the grace of the Redeemer. But perhaps it is most suitable on the Feast of his Conversion, to stop at that point, at which the day leaves him; and perhaps too it will be permitted to me on a future occasion to attempt, if it be not presumption, to speak of him again.

Meanwhile, may this glorious Apostle, this sweetest of inspired writers, this most touching and winning of teachers, may he do me some good turn, who have ever felt a special devotion towards him! May this great Saint, this man of large mind, of various sympathies, of affectionate heart, have a kind thought for every one of us here according to our respective needs! He has carried his human thoughts and feelings with him to his throne above; and, though he sees the Infinite and Eternal Essence, he still remembers well that troublous restless ocean below, of hopes and fears, of impulses and aspirations, of efforts and failures, which is now what it was when he was here. Let us beg him to intercede for us with the Majesty on high, that we too may have some portion of that tenderness, compassion, mutual affection, love of brotherhood, abhorrence of strife and division, in which he excelled. Let us beg him especially, as we are bound, to bless the most reverend Prelate, under whose jurisdiction we here live, and whose feast-day this is; that the great Name of Paul may be to him a tower of strength and fount of consolation now, and in death, and in the day of account.

SERMON VIII.

ST. PAUL'S GIFT OF SYMPATHY.

II. Cor., c. i. v. 3, 4.

Benedictus Deus et Pater Domini nostri Jesu Christi, pater misericordiarum, et Deus totius consolationis. Qui consolatur nos in omni tribulatione nostrâ, ut possimus et ipsi consolari eos qui in omni pressurâ sunt, per exhortationem quâ exhortamur et ipsi à Deo.

Blessed be the God and Father of our Lord Jesus Christ, the Father of mercies, and the God of all consolation. Who comforteth us in all tribulations, that we also may be able to comfort those who are in any distress, by the exhortation wherewith we also are exhorted by God.

THERE is no one who has loved the world so well, as He who made it. None has so understood the human heart, and human nature, and human society in its diversified forms, none has so tenderly entered into and measured the greatness and littleness of man, his doings and sufferings, his circumstances and his fortunes, none has felt such profound compassion for his ignorance and guilt, his present rebellion and his prospects hereafter, as the Omniscient. What He has actually done for us, is the proof of this. " God so loved the world, as to give His Only-begotten Son". He loved mankind in their pollution, in spite of the abhorrence with which that pollution filled Him. He loved them with a father's love, who does not cast off a worthless son once for all, but is affectionate towards his person, while he is indignant at his misconduct. He loved them for what still remained in them of their original excellence, which was in its measure a reflection of His own. He loved them before He redeemed them, and He redeemed them because He loved them. This is that " philanthropy" or "humanity" of God our Saviour, of which the inspired writers speak.

None, I say, can know the race of man so well, none can so truly love it for its own sake, as He who sent His Co-equal Son, as He who came from the Eternal Father, to save it. But His knowledge of it and His love of it arose not from any sympathy of nature, but because it was His Divine Prerogative to "know what was in man".

And, even when He became man, still He only knew by means of that Divine Omniscience, and not experimentally, the disorder of our minds and the tyranny of Satan. He was partaker indeed of our infirmities, but He could not partake of our waywardness, our passionateness, and our ignorance.

But there is a knowledge and a love of human nature, which Saints possess, which follows on an intimate experience of what human nature actually is, in its irritability and sensitiveness, its despondency and changeableness, its sickliness, its blindness, and its impotence. Saints have this gift, and it is from above; though it be gained, humanly speaking, either from the memory of what they themselves were before their conversion, or from a keen apprehension and appreciation of their own natural feelings and tendencies. And of those who have possessed it, I think the most conspicuous and remarkable instance is the great Apostle of the Gentiles; and this is a time of year when it cannot be out of place to speak of him, considering how diligent the Church is in the weeks which are now closing, to bring him before us. First, on Christmas Eve she lets us hear his voice, like some herald's trumpet, announcing again and again through the day the coming of Incarnate Grace upon earth. Then she proceeds to read his Epistles till Septuagesima; and further, not content with the feast of his Conversion, she reiterates his festival on Sexagesima, which sometimes falls on that very day, and which is a second commemoration of the Apostle. As then I have already made some remarks on his love of human nature, or philanthropy, generally, so now, on Sexagesima, I will describe it, as far as time will admit, as exercised by him within the Church, towards his Brethren,—exercised towards them, not simply as heirs of heaven, but as children of Adam, who are heirs of heaven, as possessed still of that nature as fully as before, which had to be redeemed.

He says in the text, " Blessed be the God and Father of our Lord Jesus Christ, the Father of mercies, and the God of all consolation. Who comforteth us in all our tribulations, that we also may be able to comfort those who are in any distress, by the exhortation wherewith we also are exhorted by God". Here he speaks of a ministration of charitable services, and he makes it arise out of sympathy with others; our own memory and experience of trouble urging us, and enabling us, to aid others who are in like trouble. Charity, we know, is a theological virtue, and the love of man is, properly speaking, included in the love of God. " Every one", says St. John, "that loveth Him that begot, loveth him also who is born of Him". Again, " This commandment we have from God, that he who loveth God, love also his brother". But there is another virtue distinct from charity, though closely connected with it. As Almighty God Himself has the compassion of a father on his children, " for He knoweth our frame, He remembereth that we are dust"; so, after His pattern, we are called upon to cherish the virtue of humanity, as it may be called, a virtue which comes of His supernatural grace, and is cultivated for His sake, though its object is human nature, viewed in itself, in its intellect, its affections, and its history. And it is this virtue which I consider is so characteristic of St. Paul; and he himself often inculcates it in his Epistles, as when he enjoins bowels of mercy, benignity, kindness, gentleness, and the like.

It is the habit, then, of this great Apostle to have such full consciousness that he is a man, and such love of others as his kinsmen, that in his own inward conception, and in the tenor of his daily thoughts, he almost loses sight of his gifts and privileges, his station and dignity, except he is called by duty to remember them, and he is to himself merely a frail man speaking to frail men, and he is tender towards the weak from a sense of his own weakness; nay, that his very office and functions in the Church of God, do but suggest to him that he has the imperfections and the temptations of other men.

As an apposite instance, take the passage in which, without speaking of himself in particular, he describes the sublime place which he, as well as the other Apostles, held in the Christian body. He was one of those Twelve (to use the mystical number), who were the special High-Priests of the New Testament, who sit on thrones as judges of the people, and offer before the Lamb, as Scripture speaks, golden vials, full of odours, that is, the prayers of the Saints. Yet that privilege of pontifical elevation was to him only a personal humiliation, for he himself was one of that sinful race for whom the sacrifice was offered. He contrasts all earthly High-Priests with Christ Himself, in order to bring them down to the level of their flocks. " Every High-Priest", he says, "taken from among men, is ordained for men in the things that appertain to God, that he may offer up gifts and sacrifices for sins; who can have compassion on them that are ignorant and err, because he himself also is compassed with infirmity. And therefore he ought, as for the people, so also for himself, to offer for sins". Observe his singular condescension; the one thought which his hierarchial dignity impresses on him, is that he who bears it offers sacrifice for his own sins, and ought to feel for those of others.

And when he speaks of himself and of his own office more immediately, it is in the same way. "We preach not ourselves", he says, " but Jesus Christ our Lord, and ourselves, your servants through Jesus". And then he proceeds, "We have this treasure in earthen vessels, that the excellency may be of the power of God, and not of us; always bearing about in our body the mortification of Jesus, that the life also of Jesus may be made manifest in our bodies".

His two chief scenes of labour, as far as sacred history has preserved the record, were Asia Minor and Greece. Of both countries he is especially the Apostle; but observe how he puts off the Apostle, if I may so speak, when he goes upon his Apostolic work, and rejoices to exhibit himself on that footing of human infirmity which is common to his hearers and converts, who in the order of grace and of the Church were so immeasurably his inferiors.

Speaking of his apostolic labours in Greece, he says first: "When we were come into Macedonia, our flesh had no rest; but we suffered all tribulation; combats without, fears within". Next he came down into Achaia, and his trial, and his confession of it, continue as before. "I was with you", he says to the Corinthians, "in weakness, and in fear, and in much trembling"; and this all the while that he was evidencing his Apostlic commission, as he says, "in spirit and in power". On another occasion he finds it necessary to rehearse to the same converts some of those Apostolic signs, but he is ever interrupting his catalogue with apologies for making it, and with incidental mention of his personal failings. "Although I *be* rude in speech", he says, " yet not in knowledge". "That which I speak, I speak, as it were, foolishly, in this matter of glorying". And then, after referring to his visions and ecstasies, he is not content without coming back and dwelling anew upon the infirmities he had as a man. "Lest the greatness of the revelations", he says, "should exalt me, there was given me a sting of my flesh, an angel of Satan, to buffet me. For which thing thrice I besought the Lord that it should depart from me; and He said, My grace is sufficient for thee, for power is made perfect in infirmity. Gladly, therefore, will I glory in my infirmities, that the power of Christ may dwell in me". What does all this argue in the great Apostle, but a profound self-knowledge, and an impatience lest he should not appear to his converts partaker of the same earth and ashes as themselves?

Thus he felt and spoke as regards his converts in Greece; and in Asia Minor, his manifestations, if I may so call them, are of the same kind. "I would not have you ignorant, brethren", he says, "of our tribulation, which came to us in Asia, that we were pressed out of measure, above our strength, so that we were weary even of life". And when he takes his last leave of his converts there, his language is the same; he speaks to them as an equal rather than as an Apostle, and calls them to witness that he had ever so treated them: "You know", he says to them, "from the first day I came into Asia, in what manner I have been with you for all the time, serving the Lord with all humility, and with tears, and temptations".

Now we could have easily anticipated what would be the consequence of a temper of mind so natural and so open. A man who thus divests himself of his own greatness, and puts himself on the level of his brethren, and throws himself upon the sympathies of human nature, and speaks with such simplicity and such spontaneous outpouring of heart, is forthwith in a condition both to conceive great love of them, and to inspire great love towards himself. So was it with St. Paul, and we have the evidence and record of it on that farewell visit, of which I have begun to speak, to his brethren at Ephesus, Tyre, and Cæsarea. He was leaving them for his enemies; leaving them to go to suffer at Jerusalem. What was it that was his trouble then? not the prospect of suffering, but the pain which that prospect gave to his friends. "Behold", he says, "being bound in the spirit, I go to Jerusalem, not knowing the things which shall befall me there, save that the Holy Ghost in every city witnesseth to me, saying that bonds and afflictions wait for me at Jerusalem; but I fear none of

these things". So far he is calm as well as brave.
But they earnestly besought him *not* to go up to
Jerusalem: observe the effect this had on him:
" What mean ye", he says, " weeping and afflicting my heart? for I am ready, not only to be
bound, but to die at Jerusalem, for the Name of
the Lord Jesus". You see, my Brethren, what
intimate personal attachment, what keen affection, existed between him and them. Further,
he told them that whatever happened to him,
certainly they would not see him again. "Now
behold, I know that all you, among whom I have
gone preaching the kingdom of God, shall see
my face no more. And, kneeling down, he
prayed with them all". We might have been
sure what would follow on their part: " There
was much weeping among them all; and, falling
on the neck of Paul, they kissed him, being
grieved most of all for the word that he had said,
that they should see his face no more".

There are Saints in whom grace supersedes
nature; so was it not with this great Apostle;
in him grace did but sanctify and elevate nature.
It left him in the full possession, in the full exercise, of all that was human, which was not sinful.
He who had the constant contemplation of his

Lord and Saviour, as if he saw Him with his bodily eyes, was nevertheless as susceptible of the affections of human nature and the influences of the external world, as if he were a stranger to that contemplation. Wonderful to say, he who had rest and peace in the love of Christ, was not satisfied without the love of man; he whose supreme reward was the approbation of God, looked out for the approval of his brethren. He who depended solely on the Creator, yet made himself dependent on the creature. Though he had That which was Infinite, he would not dispense with the finite. He loved his brethren, not only "for Jesus' sake", to use his own expression, but for their own sake also. He lived in them; he felt with them and for them; he was anxious about them; he gave them help, and in turn he looked for comfort from them. His mind was like some instrument of music, harp or viol, the strings of which vibrate, though untouched, by the notes which other instruments give forth, and he was ever, according to his own precept, "rejoicing with them that rejoice, and weeping with them that weep"; and thus he was the least magisterial of all teachers, and the gentlest and most amiable of all rulers. "Who is weak", he asks, " and I am not weak? who is scandalized, and I am not on fire?" And, after saying this, he characteristically adds, " If I must needs glory, I will glory of the things that concern my infirmity".

This faithful affection towards his brethren, this ardent, yet not idolatrous, love shows itself in all that he writes. For instance, we can fancy the burning desire which an Apostle must have felt to leave this scene of anguish and to be taken to enjoy the Divine Presence; yet he speaks of himself as "straitened between the two, having a desire to be dissolved and to be with Christ, a thing by far the better; but to abide still in the flesh", he continues, " is needful for you".

And when he looks forward to that happy day, when he shall receive God Himself for his reward, he associates the joys of heaven with the presence of his converts. " What is our hope, or joy, or crown of glory? Are not *you*, in the presence of our Lord Jesus Christ at His coming? for you are our glory and our joy".

And so of his friends, one by one: amid the fulness of his supernatural union with the Infinite and Eternal God, he is still ever eager for the sight of their familiar faces. "I rejoice", he says, "in the presence of Stephanas, Fortunatus, and Achaicus, for they have refreshed both my spirit and yours". Again, "I had no rest in my spirit, because I found not Titus my brother". Again, "God, who comforteth the humble, comforted us by the coming of Titus". Again, he speaks of Epaphroditus as "sick nigh unto death; but God had mercy on him, and on me also, lest I should have sorrow upon sorrow". He says with a tender lament, that "all they who are in Asia are turned away from him". For so it was, that now too, when he was about to be martyred, still, as before, he had time to think of his friends, of those who were near him, those who were away, and those who had deserted him. "At my first answer", he says, when I was first put upon trial, "no man stood with me, but all forsook me, but the Lord stood with me". "Demas hath left me, loving the present world". Luke, "the most dear physician", as he elsewhere calls him, "only Luke is with me".

I might go on in like manner, if time permitted, to remind you also how desirous he is of the approbation of his brethren:—"To God we are manifest", he says, "and I trust also to your consciences we are manifest". I might show how alive he is to slights, though at the same time most forgiving: how sensitive he is of ingratitude, though as meek and gentle as he is sensitive: how fearful he is of the effect of his punishments upon offenders, though firm in inflicting them when it is his duty: how, in short, there is not any one of those refinements and delicacies of feeling, which are the result of advanced civilization, not any one of those proprieties and embellishments of conduct in which the cultivated intellect delights, but he is a pattern of it, in the midst of that assemblage of other supernatural excellences, which is the common endowment of Apostles and Saints. He, in a word, who is the special preacher of Divine Grace, is also the special friend and intimate of human nature. He who reveals to us the mystery of God's Sovereign Decrees, manifests at the same time the tenderest interest in the souls of individuals.

And, such being his characteristics of mind, as I have been describing them, you will understand how indignant he would be sure to be, for no lighter word can be used, at the sight of jealousies, enmities, and divisions in the Christian body. He would abhor them, not only as injurious to his Saviour, but as an offence against that common nature which gives us one and all a right to the title of men. As he loved that common nature, so he took pleasure in viewing all who partake it as one, scattered though they were all over the earth. He sympathised with them all, wherever and whatever they were; and he felt it to be one special mercy, conveyed to them in the Gospel, that the unity of human nature was henceforth recognized and restored in Jesus Christ. The spirit of party, then, was simply antagonistic to the spirit of the Apostle, and a great offence to him, even when it did not go so far as schism. "Every one of you saith, I, indeed, am of Paul, and I am of Apollo, and I of Cephas, and I of Christ. Is Christ divided?" "There is neither Gentile nor Jew, Barbarian nor Scythian, bond nor free; for Christ is all, and in all".

And now I will conclude with one allusion, which it is natural for me to make, and which will justify me in saying that I have not in any great degree misconceived the Apostle's character. It is recorded of St. Philip Neri that he was specially fond of St. Paul's writings. "Of the different books of Saints", says his biographer, "he had a particular liking for the Epistles of St. Paul; in order to make his reading of them fruitful, he read slowly, and made pauses. When he felt himself warmed by what he read, he went no further, but stopped to ponder the text. When the feeling subsided, he resumed his reading, and so he went on with passage after passage". Now, we may ask at first sight what special sympathy could there be, except that they both were saints, between a humble priest, without station, without office, without extraordinary endowments of mind, and a Ruler and Doctor of the Church, a preacher, a missionary, a man of the world, and an accomplished scholar? Why did the Apostle's words come home with especial force to Philip's heart, and become food to his mind, in his small cell in the midst of a crowded city? It was, I think, because, different as the two were from each other in every other respect, in position, in gifts, and in history, they had, nevertheless, some points strikingly in common in their personal character:—these I shall sum up briefly under two heads, and so conclude.

1. And first, St. Philip Neri bears the title of

the Apostle of Rome. Why? Was he a great divine? no; he never professed any theological learning, sufficiently as he was versed in it; and it is remarkable that, great as has been the learning of many Fathers of his Congregation after him, not one of them, as far as I know, has written on a dogmatic subject, or is an authority in the sacred sciences. Did he undertake to form great saints? not so; for, leaving (as is commonly said of him) that high office for others, he turned himself in his humility to the sanctification of ordinary men. He was *not* a theologian, *not* an ascetical writer, but in a familiar way, by precept and maxim, by biographical specimens, by the lessons of history, he addressed himself to the whole community, with a view of converting all men, high and low, to God, and forming them upon the great principles, and fixing in their hearts the substance and solidity, of religious duty. He lived in an age, too, when literature and art were receiving their fullest development, and commencing their benign reign over the populations of Europe, and his work was not to destroy or supersede these good gifts of God, but, in the spirit, I may say, of a Catholic University, to sanctify poetry, and history, and painting, and music, to the glory of the Giver. Now do you not see, my Brethren, that I am but continuing my illustration of St. Paul's own character by thus speaking of the modern Saint who was his pupil? For surely St. Paul too, though an inspired Teacher, and though "nothing less than the great Apostles" in theological knowledge, nevertheless in his Epistles, instead of insisting on science and system, addresses himself chiefly to the hearts of his disciples, and introduces doctrine, not so much for its own sake, as for practical uses. And hence, though he was especially the "Doctor Gentium", yet the chief exercise of his Apostolic Office lay in forming the character and improving the heart, according to the lines of the Hymn,—

Egregie Doctor Paule, *mores* instrue,
Et nostra tecum pectora in cœlum trahe.

2. So much on St. Paul's *work:* and the latter of these two lines suggests, secondly and lastly, his *manner* of fulfilling it. Here too he was the forerunner of St. Philip. The one indeed was a ruler and a Prince in the Church, with the amplest jurisdiction; St. Philip was an obscure priest, with only the jurisdiction of a confessor;

yet the highest and the lowest agreed in this, that, putting aside forms as far as it was right to do so, and letting influence take the place of rule, and charity stand instead of authority, they drew souls to them by their interior beauty, and held them captive by the regenerate affections of human nature. St. Paul seems to have felt towards his awful Apostolic power, in some sense as David felt towards the armour of his King; and, though he used it at the call of duty, he preferred " the cords of Adam", and the voice of persuasion. What he says on one occasion to Philemon, is a sort of motto to his whole ministry. " Though I have such confidence in Christ Jesus to *command* thee that which is to the purpose, for *charity's* sake I rather *beseech*, as Paul an old man, and now a prisoner also of Jesus Christ".

No wonder then that my own Saint, being what he was, should have felt the most intimate sympathy with such a man as this; that he, who is recorded never to have said " I command" but once, and who won and guided his children by his voice and eye and look, should have felt the tenderest devotion towards the loving heart of that glorious Apostle, who was gentle on the pinnacle of the sublimest power, cheerful after ten thousand disappointments, and affectionate and sweet-tempered amid the trials of old age.

May we all of us, my Brethren, in our respective callings and stations, be partakers of this same gift, a gift which is especially needful in this age, a gift which is in singular correspondence with the duties and the objects of a University.

SERMON IX.

CHRIST UPON THE WATERS.*

Evang. sec. Matt., c. xiv. v. 24—27.

Navicula autem in medio mari jactabatur fluctibus; erat enim contrarius ventus. Quartâ autem vigiliâ noctis, venit ad eos ambulans super mare. Et videntes eum super mare ambulantem, turbati sunt, dicentes, Quia phantasma est. Et præ timore clamaverunt. Statimque Jesus locutus est eis, dicens, Habete fiduciam; ego sum; nolite timere.

The boat in the midst of the sea was tossed with the waves; for the wind was contrary. And in the fourth watch of the night He came to them, walking upon the sea. And they, seeing Him walking upon the sea, were troubled, saying, It is an apparition. And they cried out for fear. And immediately Jesus spoke to them, saying, Be of good heart; it is I; fear ye not.

THE earth is full of the marvels of divine power; "Day to day uttereth speech, and night to night showeth knowledge". The tokens of Omnipo-

* "The following sermon is written from the notes made previously to its delivery, with an attempt to preserve

tence are all around us, in the world of matter, and in the world of man: in the dispensation of nature, and in the dispensation of grace. To do impossibilities, I may say, is the prerogative of Him, who made all things out of nothing, who foresees all events before they occur, and controls all wills without compelling them. In emblem of this His glorious attribute, He came to His disciples, in the passage I have read to you, walking upon the sea,—the emblem or hieroglyphic among the ancients of the impossible; to

closely, as far as memory served, the course and matter of it, as actually delivered.

"As it has been publicly asserted, that its author has been concerned in the great measure which occasioned it, he takes this opportunity of distinctly negativing the report. It is utterly and absolutely untrue. He denies it in every shape into which it can be cast. He never was asked, and never gave, his opinion upon it, nor had he any opinion to give. He doubts whether, even in private, and to his intimate friends, he has ever expressed any sort of opinion. It was a measure in agitation before he was a Catholic. It was one of the first subjects he heard in discussion, when he became one, five years ago, and that from the lips of persons high in authority. He believes its adoption has been simply owing to the growing and full conviction of both rulers and laity in England in its favour, unattended by any suspicion whatever of its giving offence to others". — *Advertisement to First Edition.*

show them that what is impossible with man, is possible with God. He who could walk the waters, could also ride triumphantly upon what is still more fickle, unstable, tumultuous, treacherous—the billows of human wills, human purposes, human hearts. The bark of Peter was struggling with the waves, and made no progress; Christ came to him walking upon them; He entered the boat, and by entering it He sustained it. He did not abandon Himself to it, but He gathered it round Himself; He did not merely take refuge in it, but He made Himself the strength of it, and the pledge and cause of a successful passage. "Presently", another gospel says, "the ship was at the land, whither they were going".

Such was the power of the Son of God, the Saviour of man, manifested by visible tokens in the material world, when He came upon earth; and such, too, it has ever since signally shown itself to be, in the history of that mystical ark which He then formed to float upon the ocean of human opinion. He told His chosen servants to form an ark for the salvation of souls: He gave them directions how to construct it,—the length, breadth, and height, its cabins and its windows; and the world, as it gazed upon it, forthwith began to criticise. It pronounced it framed quite contrary to the scientific rules of shipbuilding; it prophesied, as it still prophesies, that such a craft was not sea-worthy; that it was not water-tight; that it would not float; that it would go to pieces and founder. And why it does not, who can say, except that the Lord is in it? Who can say why so old a framework, put together eighteen hundred years ago, should have lasted, against all human calculation, even to this day; always going, and never gone; ever failing, yet ever managing to explore new seas and foreign coasts—except that He, who once said to the rowers, "It is I, be not afraid", and to the waters, "Peace", is still in His own ark, which He has made, to direct and to prosper her course?

And hence so many instances are to be found in history, of the triumph of the bark of Peter amid adversity of every kind. "The floods have lifted up, the floods have lifted up their voice; the floods have lifted up their waves, with the noise of many waters. Wonderful are the surges of the sea; wonderful is the Lord on high". It is the Lord from heaven, who is our light in the gloom, our confidence in the storm. There is nothing hard to Him who is almighty; nothing strange to Him who is all-manifold in operation and all-fruitful in resource. The clouds break, and the sun shines, and the sea is smooth, in its appointed season. Such, my dear Brethren, is the thought which naturally possesses the mind on a day like this,[*] when we are met together solemnly to return thanks to our merciful God for the restoration of the Catholic Hierarchy to the faithful of this land. His works are ever slow and gradual; year after year brings its silent influence and contribution, in aid of the object which He may have in view; and we are unable, except artificially and for convenience, to divide into portions or stages what with Him is the continuous introduction of an integral whole. But still from time to time occur greater and more striking events, in which the past and the future are, as it were, summed up; and which, though intrinsically great, may be taken as symbols, and are representatives of even more than they are themselves, of the labours and the prospects of a course of years. And such as this is the great

[*] The Installation of the Right Rev. Dr. Ullathorne as first Bishop of Birmingham.

act which we are now commemorating: it witnesses that much has been done; it predicts that much is to follow: it is the authoritative recognition and seal of the successes which God has given us, and the instrument of their consolidation. Well, then, may we rejoice on this day; and happily does it fall on the Feast of Our Lady's Patronage, for to whom, under God, are our acknowledgments more truly due, and our expectations more securely turned, than to His all-holy and ever-glorious Mother?

Time was, my Brethren, when the forefathers of our race were a savage tribe, inhabiting a wild district beyond the limits of this quarter of the earth. Whatever brought them thither, they had no local attachments there or political settlement; they were a restless people, and whether urged forward by enemies or by desire of plunder, they left their place, and passing through the defiles of the mountains on the frontiers of Asia, they invaded Europe, setting out on a journey towards the farther west. Generation after generation passed away; and still this fierce and haughty race moved forward. On, on they went; but travel availed them not; the change of place could bring them no truth, or peace, or hope, or stability of heart; they could not flee from themselves. They carried with them their superstitions and their sins, their gods of iron and of clay, their savage sacrifices, their lawless witchcrafts, their hatred of their kind, and their ignorance of their destiny. At length they buried themselves in the deep forests of Germany, and gave themselves up to indolent repose; but they had not found their rest; they were still heathens, making the fair trees, the primeval work of God, and the innocent beasts of the chase, the objects and the instruments of their idolatrous worship. And, last of all, they crossed over the strait and made themselves masters of this island, and gave their very name to it; so that, whereas it had hitherto been called Britain, the southern part, which was their main seat, obtained the name of England. And now they had proceeded forward nearly as far as they could go, unless they were prepared to look across the great ocean, and anticipate the discovery of the world which lies beyond it.

What, then, was to happen to this restless race, which had sought for happiness and peace across the globe, and had not found it? Was it to grow old in its place, and dwindle away, and consume in the fever of its own heart, which admitted no remedy? or was it to become great by being overcome, and to enjoy the only real life of man, and rise to his only true dignity, by being subjected to a Master's yoke? Did its Maker and Lord see any good thing in it, of which, under His divine nurture, profit might come to His elect, and glory to His Name? He looked upon it, and He saw nothing there to claim any visitation of His grace, or to merit any relaxation of the awful penalty which its lawlessness and impiety had incurred. It was a proud race, which feared neither God nor man—a race ambitious, selfwilled, obstinate, and hard of belief, which would dare everything, even the eternal pit, if it was challenged to do so. I say, there was nothing there of a nature to reverse the destiny which His righteous decrees have assigned to those who sin wilfully and despise Him. But the Almighty Lover of souls looked once again; and He saw in that poor, forlorn, and ruined nature, which He had in the beginning filled with grace and light, He saw in it, not what merited His favour, not what would adequately respond to His influences, not what was a necessary instrument of His purposes, but what would illustrate and preach abroad His grace, if He took pity on it. He saw in it a natural nobleness, a simplicity, a frankness of character, a love of truth, a zeal for justice, an indignation at wrong, an admiration of purity, a reverence for law, a keen appreciation of the beautifulness and majesty of order, nay, further, a tenderness and an affectionateness of heart, which He knew would become the glorious instruments of His high will, when illuminated and vivified by His supernatural gifts. And so He who, did it so please Him, could raise up children to Abraham out of the very stones of the earth, nevertheless determined in this instance in His free mercy to unite what was beautiful in nature with what was radiant in grace; and, as if those poor Anglo-Saxons had been too fair to be heathen, therefore did He rescue them from the devil's service and the devil's doom, and bring them into the house of His holiness and the mountain of His rest.

It is an old story and a familiar, and I need not go through it. I need not tell you, my Brethren, how suddenly the word of truth came to our ancestors in this island and subdued them to its gentle rule; how the grace of God fell on them, and, without compulsion, as the historian tells us, the multitude became Christian; how, when all was tempestuous, and hopeless, and dark, Christ like a vision of glory came walking to them on the waves of the sea. Then suddenly there was a great calm; a change came over the pagan people in that quarter of the country where the gospel was first preached to them; and from thence the blessed influence went forth, it was poured out over the whole land, till one and all, the Anglo-Saxon people were converted by it. In a hundred years the work was done; the idols, the sacrifices, the mummeries of paganism flitted away and were not, and the pure doctrine and heavenly worship of the Cross were found in their stead. The fair form of Christianity rose up and grew and expanded like a beautiful pageant from north to south; it was majestic, it was solemn, it was bright, it was beautiful and pleasant, it was soothing to the griefs, it was indulgent to the hopes of man; it was at once a teaching and a worship; it had a dogma, a mystery, a ritual of its own; it had an hierarchical form. A brotherhood of holy pastors, with mitre and crosier and uplifted hand, walked forth and blessed and ruled a joyful people. The crucifix headed the procession, and simple monks were there with hearts in prayer, and sweet chants resounded, and the holy Latin tongue was heard, and boys came forth in white, swinging censers, and the fragant cloud arose, and mass was sung, and the saints were invoked; and day after day, and in the still night, and over the woody hills and in the quiet plains, as constantly as sun and moon and stars go forth in heaven, so regular and solemn was the stately march of blessed services on earth, high festival, and gorgeous procession, and soothing dirge, and passing bell, and the familiar evening call to prayer; till he who recollected the old pagan time, would think it all unreal that he beheld and heard, and would conclude he did but see a vision, so marvellously was heaven let down upon earth, so triumphantly were chased away the fiends of darkness to their prison below.

Such was the change which came over our forefathers; such was the Religion bestowed upon them, bestowed on them as a second grant, after the grant of the territory itself; nay, it might almost have seemed as the divine guarantee or pledge of its occupation. And you know its name; there can be no mistake, my Brethren; you know what that Religion was called. It was called by no modern name—for modern religions then were not. You know, my dear Brethren, *what* religion has priests and sacrifices, and mystical rites, and the monastic rule, and care for the souls of the dead, and the profession of an ancient faith, coming through all ages from the Apostles. There is one, and only one, religion such: it is known every where; every poor boy in the street knows the name of it; there never was a time, since it first was, that its name was not known, and known to the multitude. It is called *Catholicism*—a world-wide name, and incommunicable; attached to us from the first; accorded to us by our enemies; in vain attempted, never stolen from us, by our rivals. Such was the worship which the English people gained when they emerged out of paganism into gospel light. In the history of their conversion, Christianity and Catholicism are one; they are in that history, as they are in their own nature, convertible terms. It was the Catholic faith which that vigorous young race heard and embraced,—that faith which is still found, the further you trace back towards the age of the Apostles, which is still visible in the dim distance of the earliest antiquity, and to which the witness of the Church, when investigated even in her first startings and simplest rudiments, "sayeth not the contrary". Such was the religion of the noble English; they knew not heresy; and, as time went on, the work did but sink deeper and deeper into their nature, into their social structure and their political institutions; it grew with their growth, and strengthened with their strength, till a sight was seen,—one of the most beautiful which ever has been given to man to see,—what was great in the natural order, made greater by its elevation into the supernatural. The two seemed as if made for each other; that natural temperament and that gift of grace; what was heroic, or generous, or magnanimous in nature, found its corresponding place or office in the divine kingdom. Angels in heaven rejoiced to see the divinely wrought piety and sanctity of penitent sinners: Apostles, Popes, and Bishops, long since taken to glory, threw their crowns in transport at the foot of the throne, as saints, and confessors, and martyrs, came forth before their wondering eyes out of a horde of heathen robbers; guardian spirits no longer sighed over the disparity and contrast which had so fearfully intervened between themselves and the souls given to them in charge. It did indeed become a peculiar, special people, with a character and genius of its own; I will say a bold thing — in its staidness, sagacity, and simplicity, more like the mind that rules, through all time, the princely line of Roman pontiffs, than perhaps any other Christian people whom the world has seen. And so things went on for many centuries. Generation followed generation; revolution came after revolution; great men rose and fell: there were bloody wars, and invasions, conquests, changes of dynasty, slavery, recoveries, civil dissensions, settlements; Dane and Norman overran the land; yet all along Christ was upon the waters; and if they rose in fury, yet at His word they fell again and were in calm. The bark of Peter was still the refuge of the tempest-tost, and ever solaced and recruited those whom it rescued from the deep.

But at length a change again came over the land: a thousand years had well nigh rolled, and this great people grew tired of the heavenly stranger who sojourned among them. They had had enough of blessings and absolutions, enough of the intercession of saints, enough of the grace of the sacraments, enough of the prospect of the next life. They thought it best to secure this life in the first place, because they were in pos-

session of it, and then to go on to the next, if
time and means allowed. And they saw that to
labour for the next world was possibly to lose
this; whereas, to labour for this world, might be,
for what they knew, the way to labour for the
next also. Any how, they would pursue a temporal end, and they would account any one their
enemy who stood in the way of their pursuing it.
It was a madness; but madmen are strong, and
madmen are clever; so with the sword and the
halter, and by mutilation and fine and imprisonment, they cut off, or frightened away from the
land, as Israel did in the time of old, the ministers of the Most High, and their ministrations:
they "altogether broke the yoke, and burst the
bonds". "They beat one, and killed another,
and another they stoned", and at length they altogether cast out the Heir from His vineyard,
and killed Him, "that the inheritance might be
theirs". And as for the remnant of His servants
whom they left, they drove them into corners
and holes of the earth, and there they bade them
die out; and then they rejoiced and sent gifts
either to other, and made merry, because they
had rid themselves of those "who had tormented
them that dwelt upon the earth". And so they

turned to enjoy this world, and to gain for themselves a name among men, and it was given unto them according to their wish. They preferred the heathen virtues of their original nature, to the robe of grace which God had given them: they fell back, with closed affections, and haughty reserve, and dreariness within, upon their worldly integrity, honour, energy, prudence, and perseverance; they made the most of the natural man, and they "received their reward". Forthwith they began to rise to a station higher than the heathen Roman, and have, in three centuries, attained a wider range of sovereignty; and now they look down in contempt on what they were, and upon the Religion which reclaimed them from paganism.

Yes, my dear Brethren, such was the temptation of the evil one, such the fall of his victim, such the disposition of the Most High. The Tempter said, "All these will I give thee, if, falling down, thou wilt adore me"; and their rightful Lord and Sovereign permitted the boast to be fulfilled. He permitted it for His greater glory: He might have hindered it, as He might hinder all evil; but He saw good, He saw it best, to let things take their course. He did not interfere, He kept silence, He retired from the land which would be rid of Him. And there were those at that crisis who understood not His providence, and would have interfered in His behalf with a high hand. Holy men and true they were, zealous for God, and tender towards His sheep; but they divined not His will. It was His will to leave the issue to time, and to bring things round slowly and without violence, and to conquer by means of His adversaries. He willed it that their pride should be its own correction; that they should be broken without hands, and dissolve under their own insufficiency. He who might have brought myriads of Angels to the rescue, He who might have armed and blessed the forces of Christendom against His persecutors, wrought more wondrously. He deigned not to use the carnal weapon: He bade the drawn sword return to its sheath: He refused the combinations and the armaments of earthly kings. He who sees the end from the beginning, who is "justified in His words, and overcomes when He is judged", did but wait. He waited patiently; He left the world to itself, nor avenged His Church, but stayed till the fourth watch of the night, when His faithful sons had given up hope, and thought His mercy towards them at an end. He let the winds and the waves insult Him and His own; He suffered meekly the jeers and blasphemies which rose on every side, and pronounced the downfall of His work. "All things have an end", men said; "there is a time for all things; a time to be born, and a time to die. All things have their course and their term; they may last a long time, but after all, a period they have, and not an immortality. So is it with man himself; even Mathusala and Noe exhausted the full fountain of their being, and the pitcher was at length crushed, and the wheel broken. So is it with nations; they rise, and they flourish, and they fall; there is an element in them, as in individuals, which wears out and perishes. However great they may be in their day, at length the moment comes, when they have attained their greatest elevation, and accomplished their full range, and fulfilled their scope. So is it with great ideas and their manifestations; they are realized, they prevail, and they perish. As the constituents of the animal frame at length refuse to hold together, so nations, philosophies, and religions, one day lose their unity and undergo the common law of decomposition. Our nation doubtless will find its term at length, as well as others, though not yet; but that ancient faith of ours has come to nought already. We have nothing then to fear from the past; the past is not, the past cannot revive; the dead tell no tales; the grave cannot open. New adversaries we may have, but with the Old Religion we have parted once for all".

Thus speaks the world, deeming Christ's patience to be feebleness, and His loving affection to be enmity. And the faithful, on the other hand, have had their own misgivings too, whether Catholicism could ever flourish in this country again. Has it yet happened any where in the history of the Church, that a people which once lost its faith ever regained it? It is a gift of grace, a special mercy to receive it once, and not to be expected a second time. Many nations have never had it at all; from some it has been taken away, apparently without their fault, nay, in spite of their meritorious use of it. So was it with the old Persian Church, which, after enduring two frightful persecutions, had scarcely emerged from the second, when it was irretrievably corrupted by heresy. So was it with the famous Church of Africa, whose great saint and doctor's dying moments were embittered by the ravages around him of those fierce barbarians who were destined to be its ruin. What are we better than they? It is then surely against the order of Providence hitherto, that the gift once given should be given again; the world and the Church bear a concordant testimony here.

And the just Judge of man made as though He would do what man anticipated. He retired, as I have said, from the field; He yielded the battle to the enemy;—but He did so that He might in the event more signally triumph. He interfered not for near three hundred years, that His enemies might try their powers of mind in forming a religion instead of His own. He gave them three hundred years' start, bidding them to do something better than He, or something at all, if so be they were able, and He put Himself to every disadvantage. He suffered the daily sacrifice to be suspended, the hierarchy to be driven out, education to be prohibited, religious houses to be plundered and suppressed, cathedrals to be desecrated, shrines to be rifled, religious rites and duties to be interdicted by the law of the land. He would owe the world nothing in that revival of the Church which was to follow. He wrought, as in the old time by His prophet Elias, who, when he was to light the sacrifice with fire from heaven, drenched the burnt-offering with water the first time, the second time, and the third time; "and the water ran round about the altar, and the trench was filled up with water". He wrought as He Himself had done in the raising of Lazarus; for when He heard that His friend was sick, " He remained in the same place two days": on the third day He " said plainly, Lazarus is dead, and I am glad, for your sake, that I was not there, that you may believe"; and then, at length, He went and raised Him from the grave. So too was it in His own resurrection; He did not rise from the cross; He did not rise from His mother's arms; He rose from the grave, and on the third day.

So, my dear Brethren, is it now; " He hath taken us, and He will heal us; He will strike, and He will cure us. He will revive us after two days; on the third day He will raise us up, and we shall live in His sight". Three ages have passed away; the bell has tolled once, and twice, and thrice; the intercession of the saints has had effect; the mystery of Providence is unravelled; the destined hour is come. And, as when Christ arose, men knew not of His rising, for He rose at midnight and in silence, so when His mercy would do His new work among us, He wrought secretly, and was risen ere men dreamed of it. He sent not His Apostles and preachers, as at the first, from the city where He has fixed His throne. His few and scattered priests were about their own work, watching their flocks by night, with little time to attend to the souls of the wandering multitudes around them, and with no thoughts of the conversion of the country. But He came as a spirit upon the waters; He walked to and fro Himself over that dark and troubled deep; and, wonderful to behold, and inexplicable to man, hearts were stirred, and eyes were raised in hope, and feet began to move towards the Great Mother, who had almost given up the thought and the seeking of them. First one, and then another, sought the rest which she alone could give. A first, and a second, and a third, and a fourth, each in his turn, as grace inspired him,—not all together, as by some party understanding or political call,—but drawn by divine power, and against his will, for he was happy where he was, yet with his will, for he was lovingly subdued by the sweet mysterious influence which called him on. One by one, little noticed at the moment, silently, swiftly, and abundantly, they drifted in, till all could see at length that surely the stone was rolled away, and that Christ was risen and abroad. And as He rose from the grave, strong and glorious, as if refreshed with His sleep, so, when the prison doors were opened, the Church came forth, not changed in aspect or in voice, as calm and keen, as vigorous and as well furnished, as when they closed on her. It is told in legends, my Brethren, of that great saint and instrument of God, St. Athanasius, how that when the apostate Julian had come to his end, and persecution with him, the saintly confessor, who had been a wanderer over the earth, was found to the surprise of his people in his cathedral at Alexandria, seated on his episcopal throne, and clad in the vestments of religion. So is it now; the Church is coming out of prison as collected in her teaching, as precise in her action, as when she went into it. She comes out with pallium, and cope, and chasuble, and stole, and wonder-working relics, and holy images. Her bishops are again in their chairs, and her priests sit round, and the perfect vision of a majestic hierarchy rises before our eyes.

What an awful vitality is here! What a heavenly-sustained sovereignty! What a self-evident divinity! She claims, she seeks, she desires no temporal power, no secular station; she meddles not with Cæsar or the things of Cæsar; she obeys him in his place, but she is independent of him. Her strength is in her God; her rule is over the souls of men; her glory is in their willing subjection and loving loyalty. She hopes and fears nothing from the world; it made her not, nor can it destroy her. She can benefit it largely, but she does not force herself upon it. She may be persecuted by it, but she thrives under the persecution. She may be ignored, she may be silenced and thrown into a corner, but she is thought of the more. Calumniate her, and her influence grows; ridicule her,—she does but smile upon you more awfully and persuasively. What will you do with her, ye sons of men, if you will not love her, if at least you will not suffer her? Let the last three hundred years reply. Let her alone, refrain from her; for if her counsel or her work be of men, it will come to nought; but if it be of God, you cannot overthrow it, lest perhaps you be found even to fight against God.

And here I might well stop, for I have brought the line of thought which I have been pursuing to an end; but it is right to inquire how our enemies view these things, as well as how we view them ourselves; and this will lead me to ask your patient attention for a longer time.

PART II.

Ibid.

Et videntes eum super mare ambulantem, turbati sunt, dicentes, Quia phantasma est. Et præ timore clamaverunt.

And they, seeing Him walking upon the sea, were troubled, saying, It is an apparition. And they cried out for fear.

YES, my dear Brethren, would I could end at the point to which I have brought you! I ought to be able to end here: it is hard I cannot end here. Surely I have set before you a character of the Church of this day remarkable enough to attach to her the prerogatives of that divinely favoured bark in which Peter rowed, and into which the Eternal Lord entered, on the lake of Genesareth. Her fortunes during eighteen centuries have more than answered to the instance of that miraculous protection which was manifested in the fisher's boat in Galilee. It is hard that I must say more, but not strange; not strange, my Brethren, for both our Saviour's own history and His express word prepare us to expect that what is in itself so miraculous would fail to subdue, nay, would harden, the hearts of those to whom it so forcibly appeals. There is, indeed, no argument so strong but the wilful ingenuity of man is able to evade or retort it; and what happens to us in this day happened to Him also, who is in all things our archetype and forerunner. There was a time when He wrought a miracle to convince the incredulous, but they had their ready explanation to destroy its cogency. "There was offered unto Him", says the evangelist, "one possessed with a devil, both blind and dumb; and He healed him, so that he both spoke and saw. And all the multitudes were amazed, and said, Is not this the son of David? But the Pharisees hearing it, said, *This man casteth not out devils, but by Beelzebub, the prince of the devils*". So said the Pharisees; and He of whom they spoke, forewarned His disciples, that both He and His adversaries would have their respective representatives in after times, both in uttering and bearing a like blasphemy. "The disciple is not above his master", He said, "nor the servant above his lord. It is enough for the disciple that he is as his master, and the servant as his lord. *If they have called the good-man of the house Beelzebub, how much more them of His household!"*

So it was, my Brethren, that our Saviour was not allowed to point to His miracle as His warrant, but was thought the worse off for it; and it cannot startle us that we too have to suffer the like in our day. The Sinless was called Beelzebub, much more His sinful servants. And what happened to Him then, is our protection as well as our warning now: for that must be a poor argument, which is available, not only against us, but against Him. For this reason, I am not called upon to enter upon any formal refutation of this charge against us; yet it will not be without profit to trace its operation, and that I shall now proceed to do.

The world, then, witnesses, scrutinizes, and confesses the marvellousness of the Church's power. It does not deny that she is special, awful, nay, supernatural in her history; that she does what unaided man cannot do. It discerns and recognizes her abidingness, her unchangeableness, her imperturbability, her ever youthful vigour, the elasticity of her movements, the consistency and harmony of her teaching, the persuasiveness of her claims. It confesses, I say, that she is a supernatural phenomenon; but it makes short work with such a confession, viewed as an argument for submitting to her, for it ascribes the miracle which it beholds, to Satan, not to God.

This being taken for granted, as an initial assumption, from which the whole course of investigation is to proceed, and to which every result is to be referred,—viz., that the Church is not the spouse of Christ, but the child of the evil one, the sorceress described by St. John; and her supreme head, not the vicar of Christ, and pastor and doctor of His people, but the man of sin, and the destined deceiver and son of perdition,— I say, this being assumed without proof on starting, it is plain that the very evidences, which really demonstrate our divine origin, are plausibly retorted on us, as they were retorted on our Lord and Saviour, as tokens of our reprobation. Antichrist, when he comes, will be an imitative or counterfeit Christ; therefore he will *look* like Christ to the many, otherwise he would not *be* a counterfeit; but if Antichrist looks like Christ, Christ, of course, must look like Antichrist. The idolatrous sorceress, if she is to have any success in her enchantments, must feign a gravity, an authority, a sanctity, and a nobleness, which really belong to the Church of Christ alone; no wonder, then, since Satan is to be able to persuade men that she is like the Church, he is also able to persuade them that the Church is like her. Christ Himself twice was not recognized even by His disciples in the boat, who loved Him: St. Peter did not know Him after the resurrection, till St. John detected Him; and when, before this, He came walking on the sea, they at first were afraid of Him, as though He had been some evil or malignant being: " they were troubled, saying, it is an apparition, and they cried out for fear". No wonder the enemy of souls should have abundant opportunity and means of seducing the thoughtless and the headstrong, when the very Apostles, in the first years of their discipleship, were so dull in spiritual apprehension.

I say, the more numerous and striking are the evidences of the divinity of the Church, so much the more conclusively are they retorted against her, when men assume on starting that she comes, not from above, but from below. Does she claim to be sent from God? but Antichrist will claim it too. Do men bow before her, "and lick up the dust of her feet"? but, on the other hand, it is said of the apocalyptic sorceress also, that the kings of the earth shall be made "drunk with her wine". Does the Church receive the homage of "the islands, and the ships of the sea"? The answer is ready; for it is expressly said in Scripture that the evil woman shall make "the merchants of the earth rich by the abundance of her delicacies". Is the Church honoured with "the gold and frankincense of Saba, the multitude of camels, the dromedaries of Madian, and the flocks of Cedar"? Her impious rival, too, will be clothed "in purple and scarlet,' and gilded with gold", and enriched with "beasts, and sheep, and horses, and chariots". Does the Church exercise a power over the soul? The enchantress, too, will be possessed, not only of the goods of this world, but of "the souls of men". Was it promised to the sons of the Church to do miracles? Antichrist is to do "lying wonders". Do they exhibit a meekness and a firmness most admirable, a marvellous self-denial, a fervency in prayer, and a charity? It is answered: "This only makes them more dangerous. Do you not know that Satan can transform himself into an angel of light?" Are they, according to our Lord's bidding, like sheep, defenceless and patient? This does but fulfil a remarkable prophecy, it is retorted; for the second beast, which came up out of the earth, " had two horns like a lamb's, while it spoke as a dragon". Does the Church fulfil the Scripture description of being weak and yet strong, of conquering by yielding, of having nothing yet gaining all things, and of exercising power without wealth or station? This wonderful fact, which ought surely to startle the most obstinate, is assigned, not to the power of God, but to some political art or conspiracy. Angels walk the earth in vain; to the gross prejudice of the multitude their coming and going is the secret plotting, as they call it, of "monks and Jesuits". Good forsooth it cannot, shall not be; rather believe anything than that it comes from God; believe in a host of invisible traitors prowling about and disseminating doctrine adverse to your own, believe us to be liars and deceivers, men of blood, ministers of hell, rather than turn your minds, by way of solving the problem, to the possibility of our being what we say we are, the children and servants of the true Church. There never was a more success-

ful artifice than this, which the author of evil
has devised against his Maker, that God's work
is not God's but his own. He has spread this
abroad in the world, as thieves in a crowd escape
by giving the alarm; and men, in their simplicity, run away from Christ as if Christ were he,
and run into his arms as if he were Christ.

2. And if Satan can so well avail himself even
of the gifts and glories of the Church, it is not
wonderful that he can be skilful also in his exhibition and use of those offences and scandals
which are his own work in her now or in former
times. My Brethren, she has scandals, she has a
reproach, she has a shame; no Catholic will
deny it. She has ever had the reproach and
shame of being the mother of children unworthy
of her. She has good children;—she has many
more bad. Such is the will of God, as declared
from the beginning. He might have formed a
pure Church; but He has expressly predicted
that the cockle, sown by the enemy, shall remain
with the wheat, even to the harvest at the end of
the world. He pronounced that His Church
should be like a fisher's net, gathering of every
kind, and not examined till the evening. Nay,
more than this, He declared that the bad and

imperfect should far surpass the good. " Many are called", He said, " but few are chosen"; and His Apostle speaks of " a remnant saved according to the election of grace". There is ever, then, an abundance of materials in the lives and the histories of Catholics, ready to the use of those opponents who, starting with the notion that the Holy Church is the work of the devil, wish to have some corroboration of their leading idea. Her very prerogative gives special opportunity for it; I mean, that she is the Church of all lands and of all times. If there was a Judas among the Apostles, and a Nicholas among the deacons, why should we be surprised that in the course of eighteen hundred years, there should be flagrant instances of cruelty, of unfaithfulness, of hypocrisy, or of profligacy, and that not only in the Catholic people, but in high places, in royal palaces, in bishops' households, nay in the seat of St. Peter itself? Why need it surprise, if in barbarous ages, or in ages of luxury, there have been bishops, or abbots, or priests who have forgotten themselves and their God, and served the world or the flesh, and have perished in that evil service? What triumph is it, though in a long line of between two and three hundred popes, amid martyrs, confessors, doctors, sage rulers, and loving fathers of their people, one or two or three are found who fulfil the Lord's description of the wicked servant, who began " to strike the manservants and maidservants, and to eat and drink and be drunk"? What will come of it, though we grant that at this time or that, here or there, mistakes in policy, or ill-advised measures, or timidity, or vacillation in action, or secular maxims, or inhumanity, or narrowness of mind, have seemed to influence the Church's action or her bearing towards her children? I can only say that, taking man as he is, it would be a miracle were such offences altogether absent from her history. Consider what it is to be left to oneself and one's conscience, without others' judgment on what we do, which at times is the case with all men; consider what it is to have easy opportunities of sinning; and then cast the first stone at churchmen who have abused their freedom from control or independence of criticism. My Brethren, with such considerations before me, I do not wonder that these scandals take place; which, of course, are the greater in proportion as the field on which they are found is larger and wider, and the more shocking in proportion as the profession of sanctity, under which they exhibit themselves, is more prominent. What religious body can compare with us in duration or in extent? There are crimes enough to be found in the members of all denominations: if there are passages in our history, the like of which do not occur in the annals of Wesleyanism or of Independency, or the other religions of the day, recollect there have been no Anabaptist pontiffs, no Methodist kings, no Congregational monasteries, no Quaker populations. Let the tenets of Irving or Swedenborg spread, as they never can, through the world, and we should see if, amid the wealth, and power, and station which would accrue to their holders, they would bear their faculties more meekly than Catholics have done.

Come, my Brethren, I will use a very homely illustration; suffer it, if it be but apposite. You know what a sensation railway accidents occasion. Why? Because so enormous are the physical and mechanical forces which are put in motion in that mode of travelling, that, if an accident occurs, it must be gigantic. It is horrible from the conditions under which it takes place. In consequence, it impresses the imagination beyond what the reason can warrant; so that you may fall in with persons, who, on hearing, and much more, on undergoing such a misfortune, are not slow to protest that they never will travel by a railroad again. But sober men submit the matter to a more exact investigation. They do not suffer their minds to be fastened down or carried away by the thought of one or two casualties which shock them. They consider the number of lines, the frequency of trains, the multitude of passengers; they have recourse to the returns, and they calculate the average of accidents, and determine the per-centage. And then they contrast with the results thus obtained the corresponding results which coach travelling supplies, and they end, perhaps, by coming to the conclusion that, in matter of fact, the rail is safer than the road; and yet still, in spite of these undeniable facts, there are timid persons, whose imagination is more active than their reason, and who are so arrested by the exceptions, few as they are, that they cannot get themselves to contemplate the rule. In consequence they protest as steadily as before, that steam travelling is perilous and suicidal, and that they never will travel except by coach. O, my Brethren, there are many such alarmists in religion; they dress out in tract or pamphlet, they cut out and frame, some special story of tyranny, or fraud, or immorality in the long history of world-wide Catholicism, and that to them is simply Catholicism,— that to them is nothing short of a picture, a definition of Catholicism. They shrink from the great road of travel which God has appointed, and they run, as I may say, their own private conveyance, be it Wesleyanism, or Anglicanism, or Dissent, on their own track, as safer, surer, pleasanter, than the Catholic way of passage, because that passage is not secure from danger and mishap. And if this frame of mind is possible in a matter of this life, into which prejudice, and especially religious prejudice, does not enter, much more commonly and fatally will it obtain, when men are not looking for reasons to ascertain a point, but for arguments to defend it.

3. You see, my Brethren, from what I have been saying, how it is that on the one hand, the visible excellences of Catholicism do but make men suspicious of it, while on the other its scandals are sure to fill them with dread and horror. But now let me pursue the matter further; let me attempt to trace out more fully how the

English mind, in these last centuries, has come to think there is nothing good in that Religion which it once thought the very teaching of the Most High. Consider, then, this: most men, by nature, dislike labour and trouble; if they labour, as they are obliged to do, they do so *because* they are obliged. They exert themselves under a stimulus or excitement, and just as long as it lasts. Thus they labour for their daily bread, for their families, or for some temporal object which they desire; but they do not take on them the trouble of doing so without some such motive cause. Hence, in religious matters, having no urgent appetite after truth, or desire to please God, or fear of the consequences of displeasing Him, or detestation of sin, they take what comes, they form their notions at random, they are moulded passively from without, and this is what is commonly meant by " private judgment". " Private judgment" commonly means passive impression. Most men in this country like opinions to be brought to them, rather than to be at the pains to go out and seek for them. They like to be waited on, they like to be consulted for, they like to be their own centre. As great men have their slaves or their body servants for every need of the day, so, in an age like this, when every one reads and has a voice in public matters, it is indispensable that they should have persons to provide them with their ideas, the clothing of their mind, and that of the best fashion. Hence the extreme influence of periodical publications at this day, quarterly, monthly, or daily; they teach the multitude of men what to think and what to say. And thus it is that, in this age, every one is, intellectually, a sort of absolute king, though his realm is confined to himself or to his family; for at least he can think and say, though he cannot do, what he will, and that with no trouble at all, because he has plenty of intellectual servants to wait on him. Is it to be supposed that a man is to take the trouble of finding out truth, when he can pay for it? So his only object is to have cheap knowledge; that he may have his views of revelation, and dogma, and policy, and conduct,—in short of right and wrong,—ready to hand, as he has his table-cloth laid for his breakfast, and the materials provided for the meal. Thus it is, then, that the English mind grows up into its existing character. There are nations naturally so formed for speculation, that individuals, almost as they eat and drink and work, will originate doctrines and follow out ideas; they, too, of course have their own difficulties in submitting to the Church, but such is not the Englishman. He is in his own way the creature of circumstances; he is bent on action, but as to opinion he takes what comes, only he bargains not to be teased or troubled about it. He gets his opinions any how, some from the nursery, some at school, some from the world, and has a zeal for them, because they are his own. Other men, at least, exercise a judgment upon them, and prove them by a rule. He does not care to do so, but he takes them as he finds them, whether they fit together or not, and makes light of the incongruity, and thinks it a proof of common sense, good sense, strong shrewd sense, to do so. All he cares for is, that he should not be put to rights; of that he is jealous enough. He is satisfied to walk about, dressed just as he is. As opinions come, so they must stay with him; and, as he does not like trouble in his acquisition of them, so he resents criticism in his use.

When, then, the awful form of Catholicism, of which he has already heard so much good and so much evil, so much evil which revolts him, so much good which amazes and troubles him, when this great vision, which hitherto he has known from books and from rumour, but not by sight and hearing, presents itself before him, it finds in him a very different being from the simple Anglo-Saxon to whom it originally came. It finds in him a being, not of rude nature, but of formed habits, averse to change and resentful of interference; a being who looks hard at it, and repudiates and loathes it, first of all, because, if listened to, it would give him much trouble. He wishes to be let alone; but here is a teaching which purports to be revealed, which would mould his mind on new ideas, which he has to learn, and which, if he cannot learn thoroughly, he must borrow from others. The very notion of a theology or a ritual frightens and oppresses him; it is a yoke, because it makes religion difficult, not easy. There is enough of labour in learning matters of this life, without concerning oneself with the revelations of another. He does not choose to believe that the Almighty has told us so many things, and he readily listens to any person or argument maintaining the negative. And, moreover, he resents the idea of interference itself; " an Englishman's house is his castle"; a maxim most salutary in politics, most dangerous in moral conduct. He cannot bear the thought of not having a will of his own, or an opinion of his own, on any given subject of inquiry, whatever it be. It is intolerable, as he considers, not to be able, on the most awful and difficult of subjects, to think for oneself; it is an insult to be told that God has spoken and superseded investigation.

4. And, further still, consider this: strange as it may be to those who do not know him, he really believes in that accidental collection of tenets, of which I have been speaking; habit has made it all natural to him, and he takes it for granted; he thinks his own view of things as clear as day, and every other view irrational and ludicrous. In good faith and in sincerity of heart, he thinks the Englishman knows more about God's dealings with men, than any one else; and he measures all things in heaven and earth by the floating opinions which have been drifted into his mind. And especially is he satisfied and sure of his *principles;* he conceives them to be the dictates of the simplest and most absolute sense, and it does not occur to him for a moment, that objective truth claims to be sought, and a

revealed doctrine requires to be ascertained. He himself is the ultimate sanction and appellate authority of all that he holds. Putting aside, then, the indignation which, under these circumstances, he naturally feels in being invited to go to school again, his present opinions are an effectual bar to his ever recognizing the divine mission of Catholicism; for he criticizes Catholicism simply by those opinions themselves which are antagonists of it, and takes his notes of truth and error from a source which is already committed against it. And thus you see that frequent occurrence, of really worthy persons unable to reconcile their minds, do what they will, to the teaching and the ways of the Catholic Church. The more they see of her members, the more their worst suspicions are confirmed. They did not wish, they say, to believe the popular notions of her anti-christian character; but, really, after what they have seen of her authorities and her people, nothing is left to them but an hostility to her, which they are loth to adopt. They wish to think the best of every one; but this ecclesiastical measure, that speech, that book, those persons, those expressions, that line of thought, those realised results, all tend one way, and force them to unlearn a charitableness which is as pernicious as it is illusory. Thus, my Brethren, they speak; alas, they do not see that they are assuming the very point in dispute; for the original question is, whether Catholics or they are right in their respective principles and views, and to decide it merely by what is habitual to themselves is to exercise the double office of accuser and judge. Yet multitudes, of sober and serious minds and well-regulated lives, look out upon the Catholic Church, and shrink back again from her presence, on no better reasons than these. They cannot endure her; their whole being revolts from her; she leaves, as they speak, a bad taste in their mouths; all is so novel, so strange, so unlike what is familiar to them, so unlike the Anglican prayer book, so unlike some favourite author of their own, so different from what they would do or say themselves, requires so much explanation, is so strained and unnatural, so unreal and extravagant, so unquiet, nay, so disingenuous, so unfeeling, that they cannot even tolerate it. The Mass is so difficult to follow, and we say prayers so very quickly, and we sit when we should stand, and we talk so freely when we should be reserved, and we keep Sunday so differently from them, and we have such notions of our own about marriage and celibacy, and we approve of vows, and we class virtues and sins on so unreasonable a standard; these and a thousand such details are, in the case of numbers, decisive proofs that we deserve the hard names which are heaped on us by the world.

5. Recollect, too, my Brethren, that a great part of the actions of every day, when narrowly looked into, are neither good nor bad in themselves, but only in relation to the persons who do them, and the circumstances or motives under which they are done. There are actions, indeed, which no circumstances can alter; which, at all times and in all places, are duties or sins. Veracity, purity, are always virtues—blasphemy, always a sin; but to speak against another, for instance, is not always detraction, and swearing is not always taking God's name in vain. What is right in one person, may be wrong in another; and hence the various opinions which are formed of public men, who, for the most part, cannot be truly judged, except with a knowledge of their principles, characters, and motives. Here is another source of misrepresenting the Church and her servants; much of what they do admits both of a

good interpretation and a bad; and when the world, as I have supposed, starts with the hypothesis that we are hypocrites or tyrants, that we are unscrupulous, crafty, and profane, it is easy to see how the very same actions, which it would extol in its friends, it will unhesitatingly condemn in the instance of the objects of its hatred or suspicion. When men live in their own world, in their own habits and ways of thought, as I have been describing, they contract, not only a narrowness, but what may be called a onesidedness of mind. They do not judge of us by the rules they apply to the conduct of themselves and each other; what they praise or allow in those they admire, is an offence to them in us. Day by day, then, as it passes, furnishes, as a matter of course, a series of charges against us, simply because it furnishes a succession of our sayings and doings. Whatever we do, whatever we do not do, is a demonstration against us. Do we argue? men are surprised at our insolence or effrontery; are we silent? we are underhand and deep. Do we appeal to the law? it is in order to evade it; do we obey the Church? it is a sign of our disloyalty. Do we state our pretensions? we blaspheme; do we conceal them? we are liars and hypocrites. Do we display the pomp of our ceremonial, and the habits of our Religious? our presumption has become intolerable; do we put them aside and dress as others? we are ashamed of being seen, and skulk about as conspirators. Did a Catholic priest cherish doubts of his faith? it would be an interesting and touching fact, suitable for public meetings; does a Protestant minister, on the other hand, doubt of the Protestant opinions? he is but dishonestly eating the bread of the Establishment. Does a Protestant exclude Catholic books from his house? he is a good father and master; does a Catholic do the same with Protestant tracts? he is afraid of the light. Protestants may ridicule a portion of our Scriptures under the name of the Apocrypha: we may not denounce the mere Protestant translation of the Bible. Protestants are to glory in their obedience to their ecclesiastical head; we may not be faithful to ours. A Protestant layman may determine and propound all by himself the terms of salvation; we are bigots and despots, if we do but proclaim what a thousand years have sanctioned. The Catholic is insidious, when the Protestant is prudent; the Protestant frank and honest, when the Catholic is rash or profane. Not a word that we say, not a deed that we do, but is viewed in the medium of that one idea, by the light of that one prejudice, which our enemies cherish concerning us; not a word or a deed but is grafted on the original assumption that we certainly come from below, and are the servants of Antichrist.

6. Now, my dear Brethren, I have not said a word of much more that might be insisted on, and of the greatest importance. I have said not a word of the unhappy interest that men have in denying a Religion so severe against the wilful sinner as ours is:—no one likes a prophet of evil. Nor have I shown you, as I might, how natural it is, that they who sit at home and judge of all things by their personal experience of what is possible, and their private notion of what is good, should, humanly speaking, be incapable of faith in religious mysteries, such as ours. They think nothing true which is strange to them; and, in consequence, they consider our very doctrines a simple refutation of our claims. Nor, again, have I spoken of the misrepresentations and slanders with which the father of lies floods the popular mind, and which are so safe to utter, because they are, as he knows, so welcome to hear. Alas!

there is no calumny too gross for the credulity
of our countrymen, no imputation so monstrous
which they will not drink up greedily like water.
There is a demand for such fabrications, and there
is a consequent supply; our antiquity, our vastness, our strangeness, our successes, our unmove-
ableness, all require a solution; and the impostor
is hailed as a prophet, who will extemporize
against us some tale of blood, and the orator as an
evangelist, who points to some real scandal of the
Church, dead and gone, man or measure, as the
pattern fact of Catholicism. And thus it comes to
pass that we are distrusted, feared, hated, and ri-
diculed, whichever way we look; all parties, the
most hostile to each other, are still more hostile
to us, and will combine in attacking us. No one
but is brave enough to spurn us; it is no cow-
ardice to accuse us when we cannot answer, no
cruelty to fasten on us what we detest. We are
fair game for all comers. Other men they view
and oppose in their doctrines, but us they oppose
in our persons; we are thought morally and individually corrupt, we have not even natural
goodness; we are not merely ignorant of the
new birth, but are signed and sealed as the
ministers of the evil one. We have his mark

on our foreheads. That we are living beings with human hearts and keen feelings, is not conceived; no, the best we can expect is to be treated as shadows of the past, names a thousand miles away, abstractions, commonplaces, historical figures, or dramatic properties, waste ground on which any load of abuse may be shot, the convenient conductors of a distempered political atmosphere,—who are not Englishmen, who have not the right of citizens, nor any claim for redress, nor any plea for indulgence, but who are well off forsooth, if they are allowed so much as to pollute this free soil with their odious presence.

And thus we are thrown back on ourselves; for nothing we can do on the stage of the world, but is turned against us as an offence. Our most innocent actions, our attempts to please the community, our sanguine expectations of conciliating our foes, our expressions of love, are flung back upon us with scorn, to our pain and disappointment. Our simplicity, inexperience of life, ignorance of human nature, or want of tact and prudence, are put down to duplicity; and the more honest and frank are our avowals, the more certainly it is thought that a fraud lurks in the background. We are never so double-dealing as when we are candid. We are never so deep as when we have been accused and acquitted. Thus we find ourselves quite at fault how anything we do is likely to be taken, and at length, with wounded feelings, we determine to let it alone, as never knowing where to find men, or how to treat them. I have often been reminded, my Brethren, by these circumstances of ours, of the complication, not uncommon, I think, in the fictions of a popular writer who died some twenty years ago. He delights to represent innocent persons involved in circumstances which plausibly convict them of guilt, and which they are unable satisfactorily to explain. I think I recollect a young man who is accused of treason, and who, when fact after fact is brought forward to his disadvantage, conscious of his innocence, yet feeling the ingenuity of the allegation, and the speciousness of the evidence by which it is supported, and, moreover, the prejudice and cold suspicion of his judge, bursts into tears, buries his head in his hands, and refuses to answer any more interrogatories. "Do your worst", he seems to say, "not a word more shall you extract from me. You refuse to believe me; cease to question me. You are determined I am guilty; make the most of your persuasion". What is there represented in fiction happens to us in fact. We are innocent, we seem guilty, we despair of the vindication which we deserve; but we do not bury our faces in our hands, we raise our hands and our faces to our Redeemer. "As the eyes of servants are on the hands of their masters, and the eyes of the handmaid are on the hands of her mistress, so are our eyes unto the Lord our God, until He have mercy upon us. Have mercy on us, O Lord; have mercy on us, for we are greatly filled with contempt. We are a reproach to the rich and a contempt to the proud". To Thee do we appeal, O true Judge, for Thou seest us. We care not for man while we have Thee. We can afford to part with the creature while we have the Creator. We can endure "the snare of an unjust tongue, and the lips of them that forge lies", while we have Thy presence in our assemblies, and Thy witness and Thy approval in our hearts.

We do not, then, we cannot, rejoice in a mere worldly temper or in a political tone, on occasion of the event which we are celebrating to-day: no, we are too conscious both of our divine prerogatives and our high destiny, and again of the weight of that calumny and reproach which is our cross. We rejoice, not "as those who rejoice in the harvest, or as conquerors rejoice when they divide the spoils". We rejoice surely, but solemnly, religiously, courageously, as the priests of the Lord when they were carrying into battle "the ark of the Lord, the God of the whole earth". We rejoice, as those who love men's souls so well that they would go through much to save them, yet love God more, and find the full reward of all disappointments in Him; as those, whose work lies with sinners, but whose portion is with the saints. We love you, O men of this generation, but we fear you not. Understand well and lay it to heart, that we will do the work of God and fulfil our mission, with your consent, if we can get it, but, in spite of you, if we cannot. You cannot touch us except in a way of which you do not dream, by the arm of force; nor do we dream of asking for more than that which the Apostle claimed, freedom of speech, "an open door", which, through God's grace, will be "evident", though there be "many

adversaries". We do but wish to subdue you by
appeals to your reason and to your heart; give
us but a fair field and due time, and we hope to
gain our point. I do not say that we shall gain
it in this generation; I do not say we shall gain
it without our own suffering; but we look on to
the future, and we do not look at ourselves. As
to ourselves, the world has long ago done its
worst against us; long ago has it seasoned us for
this encounter. In the way of obloquy and ridicule it has exhausted upon us long since all it
had to pour, and now it is resourceless. More
it cannot say against us than it has said already. We have parted company with it for
many years; we have long chosen our portion
with the old faith once delivered to the saints, and
we have intimately comprehended that a penalty
is attached to the profession. No one proclaims
the truth to a deceived world, but will be treated
himself as a deceiver. We know our place and
our fortunes: to give a witness, and to be re-
viled; to be cast out as evil, and to succeed.
Such is the law which the Lord of all has an-
nexed to the promulgation of the truth: its
preachers suffer, but its cause prevails. Joyfully
have we become a party to this bargain; and as

we have resigned ourselves to the price, so we intend, by God's aid, to claim the compensation.

Fear not, therefore, dear Brethren of the household of faith, any trouble that may come upon us, or upon you, if trouble be God's will; trouble will but prove the simplicity of our and your devotion to Him. When our Lord walked on the sea, Peter went out to meet Him, and, "seeing the wind strong, he was afraid". Doubt not that He, who caught the disciple by the hand, will appear to rescue you; doubt not that He, who could tread the billows so securely, can self-sustained bear any weight your weakness throws upon Him, and can be your immoveable refuge and home amid the tossing and tumult of the storm. The waves roared round the Apostle, they could do nothing more: they could but excite his fear; they could but assault his faith; they could not hurt him but by tempting him; they could not overcome him except through himself. While he was true to himself, he was safe; when he feared and doubted, he began to sink. So it is now: "your adversary, the devil, as a roaring lion, goeth about": it is all he can do. So says the great Saint Antony, the first monk, who lived his long life in the Egyptian desert, and had abundant experience of conflicts with the evil one. He tells his children that bad spirits make a noise and clatter, and shout and roar, because they have nothing else to do; it is their way of driving us from our Saviour. Let us be true to ourselves, and the blustering wind will drop, the furious sea will calm. No, I fear not, my Brethren, this momentary clamour of our foe: I fear not this great people, among whom we dwell, of whose blood we come, and who have still, under the habits of these later centuries, the rudiments of that faith by which, in the beginning, they were new-born to God: who still, despite the loss of heavenly gifts, retain the love of justice, manly bearing, and tenderness of heart, which Gregory saw in their very faces. I have no fear about our Holy Father, whose sincerity of affection towards his ancient flock, whose simplicity and truthfulness I know full well. I have no fear about the zeal of the college of our bishops, the sanctity of the body of our clergy, or the inward perfection of our Religious. One thing alone I fear. I fear the presence of sin in the midst of us. My Brethren, the success of the Church lies not with pope, or bishops, or priests, or monks; it rests with yourselves. If the present mercies of God come to nought, it will be because sin has undone them. The drunkard, the blasphemer, the unjust dealer, the profligate liver,—these will be our ruin; the open scandal, the secret sin known only to God, these form the Devil's real host. We can conquer every foe but these: corruption, hollowness, neglect of mercies, deadness of heart, worldliness,—these will be too much for us.

And, O my dear Brethren, if, through God's mercy, you are among those who are shielded from these more palpable dangers and more ordinary temptations of humanity, then go on to pray for all who are in a like state with yourselves, that we may all "forget the things that are behind, and stretch forth to those that are before"; that we may "join with faith, virtue, and with virtue, knowledge, and with knowledge, abstinence, and with abstinence, patience, and with patience, pity, and with pity, love of brotherhood, and with love of brotherhood, charity". Pray that we may not come short of that destiny to which God calls us; that we may be visited by His effectual grace, enabling us to break the bonds of lukewarmness and sloth, to command our will, to rule our actions through the day, to grow continually in devotion and fervour of spirit, and, while our natural vigour decays, to feel that keener energy which comes from heaven.

SERMON X.

THE SECOND SPRING.

Cant., c. ii. v. 10—12.

Surge, propera, amica mea, columba mea, formosa mea, et veni. Jam enim hiems transiit, imber abiit et recessit. Flores apparuerunt in terrâ nostrâ.

Arise, make haste, my love, my dove, my beautiful one, and come. For the winter is now past, the rain is over and gone. The flowers have appeared in our land.

WE have familiar experience of the order, the constancy, the perpetual renovation of the material world which surrounds us. Frail and transitory as is every part of it, restless and migratory as are its elements, never-ceasing as are its changes, still it abides. It is bound together by a law of permanence, it is set up in unity; and, though it is ever dying, it is ever coming to life again. Dissolution does but give birth to fresh modes of organization, and one death is the parent of a thousand lives. Each hour, as it comes, is but a testimony, how fleeting, yet how secure, how certain, is the great whole. It is like an image on the waters, which is ever the same, though the waters ever flow. Change upon change,—yet one change cries out to another, like the alternate Seraphim, in praise and in glory of their Maker. The sun sinks to rise again; the day is swallowed up in the gloom of night, to be born out of it, as fresh as if it had never been quenched. Spring passes into summer, and through summer and autumn into winter, only the more surely, by its own ultimate return, to triumph over that grave, towards which it resolutely hastened from its first hour. We mourn over the blossoms of May, because they are to wither; but we know, withal, that May is one day to have its revenge upon November, by the revolution of that solemn circle which never stops,—which teaches us in our height of hope, ever to be sober, and in our depth of desolation, never to despair.

And forcibly as this comes home to every one of us, not less forcible is the contrast which exists between this material world, so vigorous, so reproductive, amid all its changes, and the moral world, so feeble, so downward, so resourceless, amid all its aspirations. That which ought to come to nought, endures; that which promises a future, disappoints and is no more. The same sun shines in heaven from first to last, and the blue firmament, the everlasting mountains, reflect his rays; but where is there upon earth the champion, the hero, the lawgiver, the body politic, the sovereign race, which was great three hundred years ago, and is great now? Moralists and poets, often do they descant upon this innate vitality of matter, this innate perishableness of mind. Man rises to fall: he tends to dissolution from the moment he begins to be; he lives on, indeed, in his children, he lives on in his name, he lives not on in his own person. He is, as regards the manifestations of his nature here below, as a bubble that breaks, and as water poured out upon the earth. He was young, he is old, he is never young again. This is the lament over him, poured forth in verse and in prose, by Christians and by heathen. The greatest work of God's hands under the sun, he, in all the manifestations of his complex being, is born only to die.

His bodily frame first begins to feel the power

of this constraining law, though it is the last to succumb to it. We look at the bloom of youth with interest, yet with pity; and the more graceful and sweet it is, with pity so much the more; for, whatever be its excellence and its glory, soon it begins to be deformed and dishonoured by the very force of its living on. It grows into exhaustion and collapse, till at length it crumbles into that dust out of which it was originally taken.

So is it, too, with our moral being, a far higher and diviner portion of our natural constitution; it begins with life, it ends with what is worse than the mere loss of life, with a living death. How beautiful is the human heart, when it puts forth its first leaves, and opens and rejoices in its spring-tide. Fair as may be the bodily form, fairer far, in its green foliage and bright blossoms, is natural virtue. It blooms in the young, like some rich flower, so delicate, so fragrant, and so dazzling. Generosity and lightness of heart and amiableness, the confiding spirit, the gentle temper, the elastic cheerfulness, the open hand, the pure affection, the noble aspiration, the heroic resolve, the romantic pursuit, the love in which self has no part,—are not these beautiful?

and are they not dressed up and set forth for admiration in their best shapes, in tales and in poems? and ah! what a prospect of good is there! who could believe that it is to fade! and yet, as night follows upon day, as decrepitude follows upon health, so surely are failure, and overthrow, and annihilation, the issue of this natural virtue, if time only be allowed to it to run its course. There are those who are cut off in the first opening of this excellence, and then, if we may trust their epitaphs, they have lived like angels; but wait a while, let them live on, let the course of life proceed, let the bright soul go through the fire and water of the world's temptations and seductions and corruptions and transformations; and, alas for the insufficiency of nature! alas for its powerlessness to persevere, its waywardness in disappointing its own promise! Wait till youth has become age; and not more different is the miniature which we have of him when a boy, when every feature spoke of hope, put side by side of the large portrait painted to his honour, when he is old, when his limbs are shrunk, his eye dim, his brow furrowed, and his hair gray, than differs the moral grace of that boyhood from the forbidding and repulsive aspect of his soul, now that he has lived to the age of man. For moroseness, and misanthropy, and selfishness, is the ordinary winter of that spring.

Such is man in his own nature, and such, too, is he in his works. The noblest efforts of his genius, the conquests he has made, the doctrines he has originated, the nations he has civilized, the states he has created, they outlive himself, they outlive him by many centuries, but they tend to an end, and that end is dissolution. Powers of the world, sovereignties, dynasties, sooner or later come to nought; they have their fatal hour. The Roman conqueror shed tears over Carthage, for in the destruction of the rival city he discerned too truly an augury of the fall of Rome; and at length, with the weight and the responsibilities, the crimes and the glories, of centuries upon centuries, the Imperial City fell.

Thus man and all his works are mortal; they die, and they have no power of renovation.

But what is it, my Fathers, my Brothers, what is it that has happened in England just at this time? Something strange is passing over this land, by the very surprise, by the very commotion, which it excites. Were we not near enough the scene of action to be able to say what is going on,—were we the inhabitants of some sister planet possessed of a more perfect mechanism than this earth has discovered for surveying the transactions of another globe,—and did we turn our eyes thence towards England just at this season, we should be arrested by a political phenomenon as wonderful as any which the astronomer notes down from his physical field of view. It would be the occurrence of a national commotion, almost without parallel, more violent than has happened here for centuries,—at least in the judgments and intentions of men, if not in act and deed. We should note it down, that soon after St. Michael's day, 1850, a storm arose in the moral world, so furious as to demand some great explanation, and to rouse in us an intense desire to gain it. We should observe it increasing from day to day, and spreading from place to place, without remission, almost without lull, up to this very hour, when perhaps it threatens worse still, or at least gives no sure prospect of alleviation. Every party in the body politic undergoes its influence,—from the Queen upon her throne, down to the little ones in the infant or day-school. The ten thousands of the constituency, the sum total of Protestant sects the aggregate of religious societies and associations, the great body of established clergy in town and country, the bar, even the medical profession, nay, even literary and scientific circles, every class, every interest, every fireside, gives tokens of this ubiquitous storm. This would be our report of it, seeing it from the distance, and we should speculate on the cause. What is it all about? against what is it directed? what wonder has happened upon earth? what prodigious, what preternatural event is adequate to the burden of so vast an effect?

We should judge rightly in our curiosity about a phenomenon like this; it must be a portentous event, and it is. It is an innovation, a miracle, I may say, in the course of human events. The physical world revolves year by year, and begins again; but the political order of things does not renew itself, does not return; it continues, but it proceeds; there is no retrogression. This is so well understood by men of the day, that with them progress is idolized as another name for good. The past never returns —it is never a good;—if we are to escape existing ills, it must be by going forward. The past is out of date; the past is dead. As well may the dead live to us, as well may the dead profit us, as the past return. *This*, then, is the cause of this national transport, this national cry, which encompasses us. The past *has* returned, the dead lives. Thrones are overturned, and are never restored; States live and die, and then are matter only for history. Babylon was great, and Tyre, and Egypt, and Nineve, and shall never be great again. The English Church was, and the English Church was not, and the English Church is once again. This is the portent, worthy of a cry. It is the coming in of a Second Spring; it is a restoration in the moral world, such as that which yearly takes place in the physical.

Three centuries ago, and the Catholic Church, that great creation of God's power, stood in this land in pride of place. It had the honours of near a thousand years upon it; it was enthroned in some twenty sees up and down the broad country; it was based in the will of a faithful people; it energized through ten thousand instruments of power and influence; and it was ennobled by a host of Saints and Martyrs. The churches, one by one, recounted and rejoiced in the line of glorified intercessors, who were the respective objects of their grateful homage. Canterbury alone numbered perhaps some sixteen, from St. Augustine to St. Dunstan and St. Elphege, from St. Anselm and St. Thomas down to St. Edmund. York had its St. Paulinus, St. John, St. Wilfrid, and St. William; London, its St. Erconwald; Durham, its St. Cuthbert; Winton, its St. Swithun. Then there were St. Aidan of Lindisfarne, and St. Hugh of Lincoln, and St. Chad of Lichfield, and St. Thomas of Hereford, and St. Oswald and St. Wulstan of Worcester, and St. Osmund of Salisbury, and St. Birinus of Dorcester, and St. Richard of Chichester. And then, too, its religious orders, its monastic establishments, its universities, its wide relations all over Europe, its high prerogatives in the temporal state, its wealth, its dependencies, its popular honours,—where was there in the whole of Christendom a more glorious hierarchy? Mixed up with the civil institutions, with king and nobles, with the people, found in every village and in every town,—it seemed destined to stand, so long as England stood, and to outlast, it might be, England's greatness.

But it was the high decree of heaven, that the majesty of that presence should be blotted out. It is a long story, my Fathers and Brothers

—you know it well. I need not go through it. The vivifying principle of truth, the shadow of St. Peter, the grace of the Redeemer, left it. That old Church in its day became a corpse (a marvellous, an awful change!); and then it did but corrupt the air which once it refreshed, and cumber the ground which once it beautified. So all seemed to be lost; and there was a struggle for a time, and then its priests were cast out or martyred. There were sacrileges innumerable. Its temples were profaned or destroyed; its revenues seized by covetous nobles, or squandered upon the ministers of a new faith. The presence of Catholicism was at length simply removed,—its grace disowned,—its power despised, —its name, except as a matter of history, at length almost unknown. It took a long time to do this thoroughly; much time, much thought, much labour, much expense; but at last it was done. Oh, that miserable day, centuries before we were born! What a martyrdom to live in it, and see the fair form of Truth, moral and material, hacked piecemeal, and every limb and organ carried off, and burned in the fire, or cast into the deep! But at last the work was done. Truth was disposed of, and shovelled away, and there was a calm, a silence, a sort of peace;—and such was about the state of things when we were born into this weary world.

My Fathers and Brothers, *you* have seen it on one side, and some of us on another; but one and all of us can bear witness to the fact of the utter contempt into which Catholicism had fallen by the time that we were born. You, alas, know it far better than I can know it; but it may not be out of place, if by one or two tokens, as by the strokes of a pencil, I bear witness to you from without, of what you can witness so much more truly from within. No longer the Catholic Church in the country; nay, no longer, I may say, a Catholic community;—but a few adherents of the Old Religion, moving silently and sorrowfully about, as memorials of what had been. "The Roman Catholics";—not a sect, not even an interest, as men conceived of it,—not a body, however small, representative of the Great Communion abroad,—but a mere handful of individuals, who might be counted, like the pebbles and *detritus* of the great deluge, and who, forsooth, merely happened to retain a creed which, in its day indeed, was the profession of a Church. Here a set of poor Irishmen, coming and going at harvest time, or a colony of them lodged in a miserable quarter of the vast metropolis. There, perhaps an elderly person, seen walking in the streets, grave and solitary, and strange, though noble in bearing, and said to be of good family, and—a "Roman Catholic". An old fashioned house of gloomy appearance, closed in with high walls, with an iron gate, and yews, and the report attaching to it that "Roman Catholics" lived there; but who they were, or what they did, or what was meant by calling them Roman Catholics, no one could tell;—though it had an unpleasant sound, and told of form and superstition. And then, perhaps, as we went to and fro, looking with a boy's curious eyes through the great city, we might come to-day upon some Moravian chapel, or Quakers' meeting-house, and to-morrow on a chapel of the "Roman Catholics": but nothing was to be gathered from it, except that there were lights burning there, and some boys in white, swinging censers; and what it all meant could only be learned from books, from Protestant Histories and Sermons; and they did not report well of "the Roman Catholics", but, on the contrary, deposed that they had once had power and had abused it.

And then, again, we might, on one occasion, hear it pointedly put out by some literary man, as the result of his careful investigation, and as a recondite point of information, which few knew, that there was this difference between the Roman Catholics of England and the Roman Catholics of Ireland, that the latter had bishops, and the former were governed by four officials, called Vicars-Apostolic.

Such was about the sort of knowledge possessed of Christianity by the heathen of old time, who persecuted its adherents from the face of the earth, and then called them a *gens lucifuga*, a people who shunned the light of day. Such were Catholics in England, found in corners, and alleys, and cellars, and the housetops, or in the recesses of the country; cut off from the populous world around them, and dimly seen, as if through a mist or in twilight, as ghosts flitting to and fro, by the high Protestants, the lords of the earth. At length so feeble did they become, so utterly contemptible, that contempt gave birth to pity; and the more generous of their tyrants actually began to wish to bestow on them some favour, under the notion that their opinions were simply too absurd ever to spread again, and that they themselves, were they but raised in civil importance, would soon unlearn and be ashamed of them. And thus, out of mere kindness to us, they began to vilify our doctrines to the Protestant world, that so our very idiotcy or our secret unbelief might be our plea for mercy.

A *great* change, an *awful* contrast, between the time-honoured Church of St. Augustine and St. Thomas, and the poor remnant of their children in the beginning of the nineteenth century! It was a miracle, I might say, to have pulled down that lordly power; but there was a greater and a truer one in store. No one could have prophesied its fall, but still less would any one have ventured to prophesy its rise again. The fall was wonderful; still after all it was in the order of nature;—all things come to nought: its rise again would be a different sort of wonder, for it is in the order of grace,—and who can hope for miracles, and such a miracle as this! Has the whole course of history a like to show? I must speak cautiously and according to my knowledge, but I recollect no parallel to it. Augustine, indeed, came to the same island to which the early missionaries had come already;

but they came to Britons, and he to Saxons.
The Arian Goths and Lombards too, cast off
their heresy in St. Augustine's age, and joined
the Church; but they had never fallen away
from her. The inspired word seems to imply
the almost impossibility of such a grace as the
renovation of those who have crucified to themselves again, and trodden under foot, the Son of
God. Who then could have dared to hope that,
out of so sacrilegious a nation as this is, a people
would have been formed again unto their Saviour? What signs did it show that it was to be
singled out from among the nations? Had it
been prophesied some fifty years ago, would not
the very notion have seemed preposterous and
wild?

My Fathers, there was one of your own order,
then in the maturity of his powers and his reputation. His name is the property of this diocese;
yet is too great, too venerable, too dear to all
Catholics, to be confined to any part of England,
when it is rather a household word in the mouths
of all of us. What would have been the feelings
of that venerable man, the champion of God's
ark in an evil time, could *he* have lived to see
this day? It is almost presumptuous for one

who knew him not, to draw pictures about him,
and his thoughts, and his friends, some of whom
are even here present; yet am I wrong in fancy-
ing that a day such as this, in which we stand,
would have seemed to him a dream, or, if he
prophesied of it, to his hearers nothing but a
mockery? Say that one time, rapt in spirit, he
had reached forward to the future, and that his
mortal eye had wandered from that lowly chapel
in the valley which had been for centuries in
the possession of Catholics, to the neighbouring
height, then waste and solitary. And let him
say to those about him: "I see a bleak mount,
looking upon an open country, over against that
huge town, to whose inhabitants Catholicism is
of so little account. I see the ground marked
out, and an ample enclosure made; and planta-
tions are rising there, clothing and circling in the
space. And there on that high spot, far from
the haunts of men, yet in the very centre of the
island, a large edifice, or rather pile of edifices,
appears, with many fronts and courts, and long
cloisters and corridors, and story upon story.
And there it rises, under the invocation of the
same sweet and powerful name, which has been
our strength and consolation in the Valley. I

look more attentively at that building, and I see it is fashioned upon that ancient style of art which brings back the past, which had seemed to be perishing from off the face of the earth, or to be preserved only as a curiosity, or to be imitated only as a fancy. I listen, and I hear the sound of voices, grave and musical, renewing the old chant, with which Augustine greeted Ethelbert in the free air upon the Kentish strand. It comes from a long procession, and it winds along the cloisters. Priests and religious, theologians from the schools, and canons from the Cathedral, walk in due precedence. And then there comes a vision of well nigh twelve mitred heads; and last I see a Prince of the Church, in the royal dye of empire and of martyrdom, a pledge to us from Rome of Rome's unwearied love, a token that that goodly company is firm in Apostolic faith and hope. And the shadow of the Saints is there;—St. Benedict is there, speaking to us by the voice of bishop and of priest, and counting over the long ages through which he has prayed, and studied, and laboured; there, too, is St. Dominic's white wool, which no blemish can impair, no stain can dim:—and if St. Bernard be not there, it is only that his absence may make him be remembered more. And the princely patriarch, St. Ignatius, too, the St. George of the modern world, with his chivalrous lance run through his writhing foe, he, too, sheds his blessing upon that train. And others, also, his equals or his juniors in history, whose pictures are above our altars, or soon shall be, the surest proof that the Lord's arm has not waxen short, nor His mercy failed,—they, too, are looking down from their thrones on high upon the throng. And so that high company moves on into the holy place; and there, with august rite and awful sacrifice, inaugurates the great act which brings it thither". What is that act? it is the first Synod of a new Hierarchy; it is the resurrection of the Church.

O my Fathers, my Brothers, had that revered Bishop so spoken then, who that had heard him but would have said that he spoke what could not be? What! those few scattered worshippers, *the* Roman Catholics, to form a Church! Shall the past be rolled back? Shall the grave open? Shall the Saxons live again to God? Shall the shepherds, watching their poor flocks by night, be visited by a multitude of the heavenly army, and hear how their Lord has been new born in their own city? Yes; for grace can, where nature cannot. The world grows old, but the Church is ever young. She can, in any time, at her Lord's will, "inherit the Gentiles, and inhabit the desolate cities". "Arise, Jerusalem, for thy light is come, and the glory of the Lord is risen upon thee. Behold, darkness shall cover the earth, and a mist the people; but the Lord shall arise upon thee, and His glory shall be seen upon thee. Lift up thine eyes round about, and see; all these are gathered together, they come to thee; thy sons shall come from afar, and thy daughters shall rise up at thy side". "Arise, make haste, my love, my dove, my beautiful one, and come. For the winter is now past, and the rain is over and gone. The flowers have appeared in our land......the fig-tree hath put forth her green figs; the vines in flower yield their sweet smell. Arise, my love, my beautiful one, and come". It is the time for thy Visitation. Arise, Mary, and go forth in thy strength into that north country, which once was thine own, and take possession of a land which knows thee not. Arise, Mother of God, and with thy thrilling voice, speak to those who labour with child, and are in pain, till the babe of grace leaps within them! Shine on us, dear Lady, with thy bright countenance, like the sun in his strength, *O stella matutina*, O harbinger of peace, till our year is one perpetual May. From thy sweet eyes, from thy pure smile, from thy majestic brow, let ten thousand influences rain down, not to confound or overwhelm, but to persuade, to win over thine enemies. O Mary, my hope, O Mother undefiled, fulfil to us the promise of this Spring. A second Temple rises on the ruins of the old. Canterbury has gone its way, and York is gone, and Durham is gone, and Winchester is gone. It was sore to part with them. We clung to the vision of past greatness, and would not believe it could come to nought; but the Church in England has died, and the Church lives again. Westminster and Nottingham, Beverley and Hexham, Northampton and Shrewsbury, if the world lasts, shall be names as musical to the ear, as stirring to the heart, as the glories we have lost; and Saints shall rise out of them, if God so will, and Doctors once again shall give the law to Israel, and Preachers call to penance and to justice, as at the beginning.

Yes, my Fathers and Brothers, and if it be God's blessed will, not Saints alone, not Doctors only, not Preachers only, shall be ours,—but Martyrs, too, shall re-consecrate the soil to God. We know not what is before us, ere we win our own; we are engaged in a great, a joyful work, but in proportion to God's grace is the fury of His enemies. They have welcomed us as the lion greets his prey. Perhaps they may be familiarized in time with our appearance, but perhaps they may be irritated the more. To set up the Church again in England is too great an act to be done in a corner. We have had reason to expect that such a boon would not be given to us without a cross. It is not God's way that great blessings should descend without the sacrifice first of great sufferings. If the truth is to be spread to any wide extent among this people, how can we dream, how can we hope, that trial and trouble shall not accompany its going forth? And we have already, if it may be said without presumption, to commence our work withal, a large store of merits. We have no slight outfit for our opening warfare. Can we religiously suppose that the blood of our martyrs three centuries ago and since, shall never receive its recompense? Those priests, secular and regular, did they suffer for no end? or rather, for an end which is not yet accomplished? The long imprisonment, the fetid dungeon, the weary suspense, the tyrannous trial, the barbarous sentence, the savage execution, the rack, the gibbet, the knife, the caldron, the numberless tortures of those holy victims, O my God, are they to have no reward? Are Thy martyrs to cry from under Thine altar for their loving vengeance on this guilty people, and to cry in vain? Shall they lose life, and not gain a better life for the children of those who persecuted them? Is this Thy way, O my God, righteous and true? Is it according to Thy promise, O King of saints, if I may dare talk to Thee of justice? Did not Thou Thyself pray for Thine enemies upon the cross, and convert them? Did not Thy first Martyr win Thy great Apostle, then a persecutor, by his loving prayer? And in that day of trial and desolation for England, when hearts were pierced through and through with Mary's woe, at the crucifixion of Thy body mystical, was not every tear that flowed, and every drop of blood that was shed, the seeds of a future harvest, when they who sowed in sorrow were to reap in joy?

And as that suffering of the Martyrs is not

yet recompensed, so, perchance, it is not yet exhausted. Something, for what we know, remains to be undergone, to complete the necessary sacrifice. May God forbid it, for this poor nation's sake! But still, could we be surprised, my Fathers and my Brothers, if the winter even now should not yet be quite over? Have we any right to take it strange, if, in this English land, the spring-time of the Church should turn out to be an English spring; an uncertain, anxious time of hope and fear, of joy and suffering,—of bright promise and budding hopes, yet withal, of keen blasts, and cold showers, and sudden storms?

One thing alone I know, that according to our need, so will be our strength. One thing I am sure of, that the more the enemy rages against us, so much the more will the Saints in Heaven plead for us; the more fearful are our trials from the world, the more present to us will be our mother Mary, and our good Patrons and Angel Guardians; the more malicious are the devices of men against us, the louder cry of supplication will ascend from the bosom of the whole Church to God for us. We shall not be left orphans; we shall have within us the strength of

the Paraclete, promised to the Church and to
every member of it. My Fathers, my Brothers
in the priesthood, I speak from my heart when I
declare my conviction, that there is no one
among you here present but, if God so willed,
would readily become a martyr for His sake. I
do not say you would wish it; I do not say that
the natural will would not pray that that chalice
might pass away; I do not speak of what you
can do by any strength of yours;—but in the
strength of God, in the grace of the Spirit, in
the armour of justice, by the consolations and
peace of the Church, by the blessing of the
Apostles Peter and Paul, and in the Name of
Christ, you would do what nature cannot do.
By the intercession of the Saints on high, by the
penances and good works and the prayers of the
people of God on earth, you would be forcibly
borne up as upon the waves of the mighty deep,
and carried on out of yourselves by the fulness of
grace, whether nature wished it or no. I do not
mean violently, or with unseemly struggle, but
calmly, gracefully, sweetly, joyously, you would
mount up and ride forth to the battle, as on the
rush of Angel's wings, as your fathers did before
you, and gained the prize. You, who day by

day offer up the Immaculate Lamb of God, you who hold in your hands the Incarnate Word under the visible tokens which He has ordained, you who again and again drain the chalice of the Great Victim; who is to make you fear? what is to startle you? what to seduce you? who is to stop you, whether you are to suffer or to do, whether to lay the foundations of the Church in tears, or to put the crown upon the work in jubilation?

My Fathers, my Brothers, one word more. It may seem as if I were going out of my way in thus addressing you; but I have some sort of plea to urge in extenuation. When the English College at Rome was set up by the solicitude of a great Pontiff in the beginning of England's sorrows, and missionaries were trained there for confessorship and martyrdom here, who was it that saluted the fair Saxon youths as they passed by him in the streets of the great City, with the salutation, "Salvete flores martyrum"? And when the time came for each in turn to leave that peaceful home, and to go forth to the conflict, to whom did they betake themselves before leaving Rome, to receive a blessing which might nerve them for their work? They went for a

Saint's blessing; they went to a calm old man, who had never seen blood, except in penance; who had longed indeed to die for Christ, what time the great St. Francis opened the way to the far East, but who had been fixed as if a sentinel in the holy city, and walked up and down for fifty years on one beat, while his brethren were in the battle. Oh! the fire of that heart, too great for its frail tenement, which tormented him to be kept at home when the whole Church was at war! and therefore came those bright-haired strangers to him, ere they set out for the scene of their passion, that the full zeal and love pent up in that burning breast might find a vent, and flow over, from him who was kept at home, upon those who were to face the foe. Therefore one by one, each in his turn, those youthful soldiers came to the old man; and one by one they persevered and gained the crown and the palm,—all but one, who had not gone, and would not go, for the salutary blessing.

My Fathers, my Brothers, that old man was my own St. Philip. Bear with me for his sake. If I have spoken too seriously, his sweet smile shall temper it. As he was with you three centuries ago in Rome, when our Temple fell, so now surely when it is rising, it is a pleasant token that he should have even set out on his travels to you; and that, as if remembering how he interceded for you at home, and recognizing the relations he then formed with you, he should now be wishing to have a name among you, and to be loved by you, and perchance to do you a service, here in your own land.

SERMON XI.

ORDER, THE WITNESS AND INSTRUMENT OF UNITY.

Evang. sec. S. Luc., *c.* ix. *v.* 2–4.

Et misit illos prædicare regnum Dei, et sanare infirmos. Et ait ad illos: nihil tuleritis in via, neque virgam, neque peram, neque panem, neque pecuniam; neque duas tunicas habeatis. Et in quamcumque domum intraveritis, ibi manete, et inde ne exeatis.

And He sent them to preach the kingdom of God, and to heal the sick. And he said to them: Take nothing for your journey, neither staff, nor scrip, nor bread, nor money; neither have two coats; and whatever house you shall enter into, abide there, and depart not from thence.

THESE words, taken from the Gospel which has just now found a place in the sacred solemnity in which we are at present engaged, may be called the ceremonial, with which the preachers of the New Law were ordered to go forward for the execution of their charitable work. In this point of view, as in other respects, they are remarkable words, as intimating to us how utterly contrary it is to the character and spirit of the Divine Appointments to do anything without order and prescription. If an occasion could be supposed on which external forms might have been dispensed with, surely it was then, when the Disciples were to be wanderers on the face of the earth, to be whirled about as leaves by the rude blast, and to be accounted fortunate if they managed in their mission to secure themselves from torture and death. Yet even on that their first entrance into the regions of darkness and sin, ere the faithful had grown into an extended, and formed into an organized body, ere they had secured vigour and weight sufficient to act upon the world, even in the Church's initiatory and provisional state, we find her furnished by her Divine Founder with canons and decrees for the first simple movements and actions of her ministers. Even in those rudimental efforts, the Apostle's rule is to be verified: "Non est dissentionis Deus sed pacis". He is not a God of confusion, of discordance, of accidental, random, private courses in the execution of His will, but of determinate, regulated, prescribed action. It might have seemed a matter of indifference how the

Disciples addressed themselves to their missionary work; but no, they were to go forth "in pace, et in nomine Domini": their very dress, their carriage, and their journeying, were anticipated for them, and were to be of one kind, not of another.

All the works of God are founded on unity, for they are founded on Himself, who is the most awfully simple and transcendent of possible unities. He is emphatically One; and whereas He is also multiform in His attributes and His acts, as they present themselves to our minds, it follows that order and harmony are of His very essence. To be many and distinct in His attributes, yet, after all, to be but one,—to be sanctity, justice, truth, love, power, wisdom, to be at once each of these as fully as if He were nothing but it, as if the rest were not,—this implies in the Divine Nature an infinitely sovereign and utterly incomprehensible order, which is an attribute as wonderful as any, and the result of all the others. He is an infinite law, as well as an infinite power, wisdom, and love. Moreover, the very idea of order implies the idea of the subordinate. If order exists in the Divine Attributes, they must have relations one to another, and though each is perfect in itself, it must act so as not to impair the perfection of the rest, and must seem to yield to the rest on particular occasions. Thus God's power, indeed, is infinite, but it is still subordinate to His wisdom and His justice; His justice, again, is infinite, but it, too, is subordinate to His love; and His love, in turn, is infinite, but it is subordinate to His incommunicable sanctity. There is an understanding between attribute and attribute, so that one does not interfere with the other, for each is supreme in its own sphere; and thus an infinitude of infinities, acting each in its own order, are combined together in the infinitely simple unity of God.

Such is the unity, and consequent harmony and beauty, of the Divine Nature, even when viewed in the lights which are supplied to us by the traditions of the human race and the investigations of the human intellect. But, wonderful as is that order and harmony, considered only in the way of nature, much more wonderful is it in the mysteries of Revelation. There we are introduced to the ineffable, the adorable, the most gracious dogma of a Trinity in Unity, which is what I may call the triumph of Unity over difficulties, which, to our limited faculties, seem like impossibilities and contradictions. How strong, how severe, how infinitely indivisible, must be that Unity of God, which is not compromised by the truth of His being Three! How surpassing is that Unity of substance which remains untroubled and secure, though it is occupied and possessed wholly and unreservedly, not only by the Father, but also by the Son; not only by Father and Son, but by the Holy Ghost also! And, moreover, as there is a subordination, as I have said, of attribute to attribute, without any detriment to the infinitude of each of them individually, and this is the glory of the God of Nature; so also does an order, and, as I may say, a subordination exist between Person and Person, and this is the incommunicable glory of the God of Grace. Father, Son, and Holy Ghost, are all equal to Each Other in their Divinity, else They would not Each be the One God. Yet, true as it is, that not one of the Divine Persons is less infinite, less eternal, less all-sufficient than the Other Two, it is true also that, in the history of the Everlasting Mystery, the Father comes first in order, as the Fountain-head of Divinity; the Son second, as being the Offspring of the

First; and the Holy Ghost third, as proceeding from the Father and the Son. And for this reason it would appear that the Second and Third Persons hold certain offices, such as that of mission, which are fitting only in Them. Hence it was fitting that the Son should be Incarnate, and not the Father; and fitting that the Holy Ghost should be the energizing life, both of the animate and rational creation, and not the Father or the Son.

Nay, further than this still: so dear to Almighty God is that principle of order and of law, which is a characteristic of His glorious Essence, that, when He would reveal Himself to man, He even placed Himself under the conditions of an additional law, which did not belong to His nature, but was the mere creation of His will. He limited, as I may say, the range of His omnipotence by the obligation of His promise. Considered in Himself, He is, of course, in no respect a debtor to His creatures, nor answerable to them; there was no justice that could exist between them and Him; they could not profit Him, nor claim anything of Him; they were, in Our Lord's words, but "servi inutiles"; yet the Almighty, after wonderfully calling into existence the rational creation, has more wonderfully placed it on a level with Himself. He has invested it with rights and titles. He has given it a power of meriting, and a ground for encountering and influencing His own determinations and acts. Henceforth, not only are His creatures bound, but He also. "Dimitte Me", He said to Moses, on his pleading for Israel; "Let Me go", "Set Me free", "Do not stand in the way of My will", "Dimitte Me ut irascatur furor meus contra eos", "that My wrath may be kindled against them". He was restrained in the exercise of His attribute of justice by the necessity of faithfulness to His word; but what I remark is, that unless the notion of law, and of subjection to it, were elementary to the idea of the Divine Being, He never would have previously placed Himself in what (as in this instance) may be called a state of restraint. He voluntarily made promises and put Himself under engagements, from it being of His very nature to love order, and rule, and subordination for their own sake.

Such being the teaching, both of nature and of grace, concerning the Almighty, it is not surprising that, whereas in all things our blessedness

lies in being like Him, in this respect especially
His pattern should be our duty and our good.
The God of order has set up all creation upon
unity, and therefore upon law. Time was when
philosophists contended that all things went on
at random; that the phenomena of the material
world were the result of the blind dance of
everlasting atoms, and that the beauty on the
face of nature was no earnest or evidence of the
existence of any systematic plan of which it was
the result. Such a fancy is now simply despised
and abandoned even by those who do not recognize the Divine Creator in His works. Even
those who have no eyes to see the Omniscient
and the Omnipotent, now ridicule and repudiate
the idea of chance and hazard in the course of
physical nature; for the further their investigations are carried into the material framework
of the universe, the more certain is the existence, the more encompassing is the range, of
order and of law. There is no unrestrained, no
lawless freedom in the physical world,—after the
pattern of its Maker. It is not, indeed, good as
He is good, even in its own degree; for it is full
of fault and imperfection, and might be better
than it is. It is not wise as He is wise; rather

it has no intelligence at all lodged in it. It is not stable as He is stable; but, on the contrary, it is ever in motion and ever on the change. But one attribute it has of God, without exception or defect, and that is the attribute of order. Here it is as perfect in its finite degree and after its kind, it is as simply the manifestation of harmony and of law, as the infinite Creator Himself.

And so of the rational creation also, both in heaven and upon earth. The Angels have their hierarchy above; distributed into nine orders, they hymn the praises, and they fulfil the will, of the Omnipotent. And here below the history of mankind is founded upon the existence of society, and before and without formed political bodies there is no course of events to record. While men remain as savages, there is nothing to tell of them; nor is this all;—but the more accurately the history of the world can be investigated and put into shape, the more does it evidently appear to advance upon fixed laws, both as regards time and place, though, of course, without interfering with the responsibility of the individual.

But amongst all the instances of unity, of harmony, and of law, which the Creator has given us after His own image, the most remarkable is that which He set up when He came upon earth, the most perfect is that which exists in His Church. In the awful music of her doctrines, in the deep wisdom of her precepts, in the majesty of her Hierarchy, in the beauty of her Ritual, in the dazzling lustre of her Saints, in the consistent march of her policy, and in the manifold richness of her long history,—in all of these we recognize the Hand of the God of order, luminously, illustriously displayed. In her whole and in her parts, in her diversified aspects, the one same image of law and of rule ever confronts us; as in those crystallized substances of the physical world, which, both in the mass and in the details, consist in a reiteration of one and the same structure.

My Brethren in the Sacred Ministry, you see to what conclusion I am conducting the train of thought which I have been pursuing. We, indeed, by virtue of that ministry, are at all times subjects and guardians of that Sacramentum Unitatis, which the Holy Fathers have ever recognized as lodged in the Church of God. Such we are by our office under all circumstances;—but, if there be a time when we are preëminently witnesses of this great and eternal truth, it is not when we are performing one by one our daily duties, though even then we represent in our individual persons the unity of her teaching and of her rule;—nor is it even when we offer Mass amid our own people, though then, indeed, we formally unite and seal them all with the impress of the One God, the One Mediator, the One Sacrifice for sin once offered, and the One Faith, —but it is surely at those special and rare seasons, of which the present is one, when all ranks and orders of the elect household are brought together from all parts into one place, under the invocation of One Spirit, in the form of a visible hierarchy, and as an image of the whole Catholic Church;—when the Bishop in his cathedral and on his throne, the Clergy who share his counsels and his anxieties, the Pastors who are deputed from him to feed his flock in every place, the Regulars whom Christ's own Vicar has sent to minister to him in his incessant toils, the ecclesiastics of inferior rank, the students from the Seminary, and the faithful people in attendance, when all are thus brought together in the august form of Synod, and in the solemnity of its prescribed ceremonial: and still more, if more need be said, when such a meeting of the Church has the singular and most touching prerogative of being the first which has been held through a long three hundred years, and is the token of a change of times, and of a resurrection in this island, of the fair presence of Catholicism.

My Reverend Brethren, under such circumstances is it wonderful that my mind recurs to the history and the teaching of a great servant of God, of a primitive Bishop and Martyr, whose lot was cast in a day, which, as regards the particular subject before us, may be parallelled to our own? In the beginning of the New Dispensation, things were in that provisional state, which I touched upon when I began;—not as if the dogma and the rule of the Church could be different at one time and at another, but "Hæc omnia operatur unus atque idem Spiritus, dividens singulis, prout vult"; "All these things one and the same Spirit worketh, dividing to every one according as He will". From the first, indeed, as ever, there was but one source of ecclesiastical jurisdiction; from the first, one Pastor

Ordinarius of all the faithful; from the first, bishops had their thrones in the Church, of divine right; from the first, the hierarchy was determined;—but not from the first were all these appointments observed with the exactness which they admitted and required. At first, twelve, and not one, were possessed of universal jurisdiction; at first bishops and priests, though ever separate in their office, were not always separate in their work and their position; at first, those who were called to follow the evangelical counsels, observed them, not in community, nor in solitude, but in the bosom of their families. In these, and many other ways, the visible Church, though set up from the first in its substance, was not from the first manifested in the fulness of operation and institution.

But, when the last Apostle had been taken to his throne above, and the oracle of inspiration was for ever closed, when the faithful were left to that ordinary government which was intended to supersede the special season of miraculous action, then arose before their eyes in its normal shape and its full proportions that majestic Temple, of which the plans have been drawn out from the first by our Lord Himself amid His elect Disciples. Then was it that the Hierarchy came out in visible glory, and sat down on their ordained seats in the congregation of the faithful. Then followed in due course the holy periodical assemblies, and the solemn rites of worship, and the honour of sacred places, and the decoration of material structures; one appointment after another, realizing in act and deed the great idea which had been imparted to the Church since the day of Pentecost. Then, in a word, was it that the Church passed from what I may call the Apostolic Vicariate, to its true form of Diocesan Episcopacy, which whoso destroys, as a Pope and Doctor especially dear to English Catholics has intimated, is the forerunner of Antichrist.

And this change of government took place, not because persecution had ceased, not because the powers of the world gave leave, but because it seemed good to the Holy Ghost, for the welfare of the faithful, at that very time to bind together, in every part of the Church, ruler and subjects, into a closer and more loving unity. And so, as a beginning and in encouragement of the good work, the same Divine Providence at that very time sent her a glorious martyr, St. Ignatius of Antioch, to be her prophet and doctor,—as in regard to the doctrine of the Incarnation, as in regard to the science of the saints,—so preëminently as regards the structure and the sacramental power of the Ecclesiastical Hierarchy. Welcome and cheering did his words sound in the ears of those early Christians, as they were wafted to them while he travelled along to martyrdom. Suitably and seasonably do they speak to us at present, who are now assisting in the same ecclesiastical revolution which was in progress then. Appositely, surely, and without apology, I may now quote some portion of them, as a fit comment on the ceremonial of these days.

"Jesus Christ", he says to the Ephesians, "our true Life, is the Mind of the Father; and so the Bishops, appointed even to the utmost bounds of the earth, are after the mind of Jesus Christ. Wherefore it will become you to concur in the mind of your Bishop, as also ye do. For your famous Presbytery, worthy of God, is knit as closely to its Bishop as the strings to a harp. Therefore by your unanimity and harmonious love, Jesus Christ is sung; and each of you taketh part in the chorus. Wherefore, it is profitable for you to live in blameless unity, that so ye may always have fellowship with God. Let no man deceive himself; if he be not within the Altar, he faileth of the Bread of God. For, if the prayer of one or two be of such force, as we are told, how much more that of the Bishop and the whole Church? He therefore that does not come together into the same place with it, is proud, and has already condemned himself. Let us take heed, then, not to set ourselves against the Bishop, that we may be subject to God. And the more any one seeth his Bishop keep silence, the more let him reverence him; for whomsoever the Master of the house sends to be over His own household, we ought to receive him, even as we would Him that sent him. It is plain, therefore, that we ought to look to the Bishop, even as to the Lord Himself".

To the Magnesians: "Meet it is, that for the honour of Jesus Christ, the Bishop of us all,* who wills it, that ye should preserve an obedience that is without guile; since a man does not deceive the Bishop whom he sees, but he practises rather with the Bishop invisible, and so the question is not with flesh, but with God, who knows the secret heart".

To the Trallians: "He that is within the Altar

* Parts of two sentences are put together here.

is pure; but he that is without is not pure. That is, he that doeth anything without the Bishop and the Presbyters and Deacons, is not pure in his conscience".

To the Philadelphians: "Although some would have deceived me according to the flesh, yet the spirit is not deceived, being from God. For it knows both whence it comes, and whither it goes, and reproves the secret heart. I cried whilst I was among you, I spoke with a loud voice: Give ear to the Bishop, and to the Presbytery and to the Deacons. And some suppose that I spake this, as knowing beforehand the separation of some. But He is my witness, for whose sake I am in bonds, that I knew nothing from any man. But the Spirit spake, saying in this wise: Do nothing without the Bishop; keep your bodies as the temples of God; love unity; flee divisions; be followers of Christ, as He of His Father".

May we all learn from the parting words of one, who warned us, as I may say, in the very agonies of martyrdom, to advance more and more in the spirit of obedience, in brotherly affection, in mutual forbearance and concession, in sympathy and compassion one for another. "In humilitate superiores sibi invicem arbitrantes", says the Apostle, "non quæ sua sunt singuli considerantes, sed ea quæ aliorum. Supportantes invicem, et donantes vobismet ipsis, si quis adversus aliquem habet querelam". "In humility, esteeming others better than themselves: each one not considering the things that are his own, but those that are other men's; bearing with one another, and forgiving one another, if any have a complaint against another". The world looks upon us as a political, crafty, grasping set of men, like its own children. It recognizes, in the establishment of our Hierarchy, the work of an ambitious aspiration; and thinks us bound together by mere earthly bonds, by selfishness, by expedience, by party spirit, by servile fear, and by ignorance. It knows nothing (how can it know?) of that hidden life, of that faith, that love, that spirit of adoration, which is our incorporating principle. It knows nothing of that Divine Presence, which, when It left the earth visibly, told us that we should still possess It, though the world would not. It has no experience of the operations of grace, of the efficacy of the Sacraments, of the power of prayer, of the virtue of holy relics, of the communion of Saints, of the glorious intercession of the Mother of God, and of the care and tenderness of the Guardian Angel. It takes for granted, that what it sees, and just as much as it sees, is the whole of us. *We* know, my dear and reverend Brethren, we know, we witness to each other, and to God, in calm and thankful confidence, that we have that which the world does not dream of. We know well, that in all these matters which, during the last several years, have brought the wrath of man upon us, in the establishment of the Hierarchy and the celebration of Synods, we have but been aiming to do God's will more perfectly. We know well, that we have acted as those, who one day must give account for their gifts and their works before the awful judgment seat; and that what the world takes for ambition or craft, has been but an effusion of love.

You, my Lord and Father, are by these very changes,—by becoming the Bishop of an English Diocese, and no longer the Vicar of the Holy See, sent hither for the charge of the faithful,—you are circumscribing your power, and laying yourself under obligations which before you had not. Now no longer the mere representative of him who has the plenitude of jurisdiction, but as the shepherd of a flock, you are bound to your clergy and people, you are knit into the body of the faithful, whom you rule and whom you serve, by a more intimate tie, and a severer liability. Not only in will and in intention, but from your office and your position, henceforth you will be taking no measures by yourself, but with the counsel of others, as well as for their well-being. As the Eternal placed Himself under the conditions of a compact, when He would reveal Himself to sinful man, as He made Himself subject to the law of human nature when He took human flesh, so do the diocesan obligations which you have undertaken make you less free than you were before, and, from love to the souls of your priests and your people, do you rejoice in such captivity.

And still more is this true, my Reverend Brethren, of each of us, the Bishop's children and servants, each in his own place. We are no longer solitary labourers in our several spheres, cut off from our brethren, and at a distance from our head. We are, in a sense, in which we were not before, members of a body. We are participating in a special way in the great Sacramentum Unitatis, and are bringing ourselves thereby nearer to the Divine Source of truth, purity, and charity, who lives in that visible form. We are met here to gain grace, and instruction, and consolation, and encouragement, from the One Eternal Bishop of the Church, whom our visible Father and Head represents. We are come that that celestial order and peace, and that perfection of law, and that hierarchy of gifts and virtues, of which the Church is the manifestation, may also be set up and manifested, according to our measure, in our own persons. We come here to go back more able to govern ourselves, and to do God's will, and to preach His word, and to be a pattern to His people.

Yes! if there be on earth a visible image of heaven, it is in the Church collected together in one place; and we come here to drink, from that present source of grace, the strength and health and vigour needful for us on our journey thither. When even a fallen servant of God and his satellites entered the company of prophets under the Old Law, and saw them prophesying, and Samuel standing over them, the Spirit of God came upon the intruders, and they too began to prophesy. Again, under the New Law, when even an unbeliever came into the assemblies of the infant Church, (an Apostle is our warrant for saying it,) he was overcome and transformed by the harmony of her worship. Her very presence and action was the sufficient note of her divinity. What, then, my Reverend Brethren, will not be the influence of her ceremonial on us, who, erring though we be as mortal men, still, as we trust, have the grace of God within us, are aiming after meekness, purity, charity, and detachment from the world, and are faithfully though imperfectly fulfilling the high commission severally given to us? May we not believe, through the mercy of Him who has chosen us, that we shall carry back with us a something which hitherto we had not?—a fuller and deeper view of the great dispensation of which we are the ministers, a clearer understanding of the beauty of God's House, a firmer faith in the solidity of that rock on which it stands, a closer devotion to Him who inhabits it, a more subdued, more peaceful, and more happy temper, to encounter the trials which meet us on our course, and which are appointed to lead us forward to heaven.

SERMON XII.

THE MISSION OF ST. PHILIP NERI.

Eccli., *c.* xxxiii. *v.* 16-18.

Et ego novissimus evigilavi, et quasi qui colligit acinos post vindemiatores. In benedictione Dei et ipse speravi, et quasi qui vindemiat, replevi torcular. Respicite quoniam non mihi soli laboravi, sed omnibus exquirentibus disciplinam.

I awaked last of all, and as one that gathereth after the grape-gatherers. In the blessing of God I also have hoped; and as one that gathereth grapes, have I filled the wine-press. See that I have not laboured for myself only, but for all that seek discipline.

THE Picture of St. Philip is ever in this Chapel, and his image is ever in our minds. Not only we, who belong to his Congregation, and have devoted ourselves to his service, but you, my dear Brethren and Children, who come to worship here under his shadow, you, too, I am persuaded, carry him away with you to your homes, and find by experience the benefit of such a Patron. His commemoration is of daily wont in this neighbourhood, and the Octave of his Festival runs round the full circuit of the year. At no season is it necessary to remind you of him; nor at this particular season is there any special reason, either from ritual or from custom, which makes it suitable or dutiful to do so. And yet, in our own case it is more natural to think and speak of him at this time than at any other, for we are approaching the anniversary of his coming into England and into Birmingham, and are returning thanks to our good God in a series of devotions, for all the mercies which, through his intercession, have, in the course of two years, been poured out upon us. We are now close upon completing the second year since the first introduction* of the Oratory into England; close upon completing the first, since it took up its abode in this populous town,† to which the Apostolical Brief sent it. Our prospects we know surely, will extend, and our successes multiply, as time goes on; and we may be enabled to furnish the elements, or to lay the rudiments of Oratories for other places; but, if the proverb be true, that "he who begins,

* February 2, 1848. † Birmingham.

does half the work", we had a mercy shown us this time year, the like of which we never can have shown us again.

Nor do we at this season turn only in gratitude to our dear Saint and Father, for what he has gained for us: we turn to him, also, as our most necessary pattern in the return which it is our duty to make to God for it. He who has gained for us God's mercies, he, my dear Fathers of the Oratory, must teach us to use them worthily; and this leads us to think over and dwell both on him and on his history, as though it were now his yearly festival;—to enlarge upon the special traits of his character and memorable passages of his life, if not for his sake, at least for our own; if not to do him honour, at least to gain guidance for ourselves, by reason of the light which all that is recorded of him casts upon our vocation, our duties, and our work; for then only are we his true followers, when we do as he did. Moreover, although all this is a subject of thought which concerns us, the members of the Oratory, primarily, yet it must have an interest for those also who, like yourselves, my Brethren, make use of our ministrations; for, whereas there are many professions, missions, and undertakings in the length and breadth of the Catholic Church, you will, by considering it, understand more exactly what it is in particular, that the Oratory proposes to do for you.

Let us, then, inquire what St. Philip's times were, and what place he holds in them; what he was raised up to do, how he did it, and how we, my Fathers of the Oratory, may make his work and his way of doing it a pattern for ourselves in this day.

His times were such as the Church has never seen before nor since, and such as the world must last long for her to see again; nor peculiar only in themselves, but involving a singular and most severe trial of the faith and love of her children. It was a time of sifting and peril, and of "the fall and resurrection of many in Israel". Our gracious Lord, we well know, never will forsake her; He will sustain her in all dangers, and she will last while the world lasts; but if ever there was a time when He seemed preparing to forsake her—it was not the time of persecution, when thousands upon thousands of her choicest were cut off, and her flock decimated; it was not in the middle age, when the ferocity of the soldier and subtlety of the sophist beleaguered her,—but it was in that dreary time, at the close and in the fulness of which St. Philip entered upon his work. A great author, one of his own sons, Cardinal Baronius, has said of the dark age, that it was a time when our Lord seemed to be asleep in Peter's boat; but there is another passage of the Gospel still more wonderful than the record of that sleep, and one which had a still more marvellous accomplishment in the period of which I have to speak. There was a time when Satan took up bodily the King of Saints, and carried Him whither he would. Then was our most Holy Saviour and Lord clasped in the arms of ambition, avarice, and impurity:—and in like manner His Church also after Him, though full of divine gifts, the Immaculate Spouse, the Oracle of Truth, the Voice of the Holy Ghost, infallible in matters of faith and morals, whether in the chair of her Supreme Pontiff or in the unity of her Episcopate, nevertheless was at this time so environed, so implicated, with sin and lawlessness, as to appear in the eyes of the world to be what she was not. Never, as then, were her rulers, some in higher, some in lower degree, so near compromising what can never be compromised; never so near denying in private what they taught in public, and undoing by their lives what they professed with their mouths; never were they so mixed up with vanity, so tempted by pride, so haunted by concupiscence; never breathed they so tainted an atmosphere, or were kissed by such traitorous friends, or were subjected to such sights of shame, or were clad in such blood-stained garments, as in the centuries upon and in which St. Philip came into the world. Alas for us, my Brethren! the scandal of deeds done in Italy then is borne by us in England now.

It was an age when the passionate wilfulness of the feudal baron was vigorous still; when civilization, powerless as yet to redress the grievances of society at large, gave to princes and to nobles as much to possess as before, and less to suffer; increased their pomp, and diminished their duties and their risks; became the cloak of vices which it did not extirpate, made revenge certain by teaching it to be treacherous, and unbelief venerable by proving it to be ancient. Such were the characteristics of St. Philip's age; and Florence, his birth-place, presented the most complete exhibition of them,—and next to Florence, Rome, the city of his adoption.

Florence was at that time the most intellectual, the most magnificent city of Italy. About a century before, one of its richest merchants and bankers* had become its virtual ruler, and had transmitted his power to his descendants, who still possessed it. The history of this family is intimately connected with that of the Holy See; at times they were its enemies: they ended in giving to it three or four princes of their own blood to fill it: but whether in alliance with it or at war, whether at Florence or at Rome, they exerted, at least for many years, an influence prejudicial to its real, that is, its religious well-being.

This was the time of the revival of what is called classical learning; that is, the learning of ancient Greece and Rome. Constantinople had lately been taken by the Turks, who still hold it; its scholars, with their traditions and their manuscripts, escaped to Italy, and they found a home at Florence with this powerful family. Its representatives became the special patrons of

* Cosmo de' Medici.

Literature and the Arts, and leaders of the classical revival. Under their auspices, public schools were opened; the Greek language was studied; an Academy was established for philosophy; a library was founded, and placed in the Dominican Convent of St. Mark. Its librarian in course of time became Pope,* and founded at Rome the famous Vatican Library. Books in the languages of the East,—Hebrew, Arabic, even Indian, were collected; the lost writings of Greek and Roman authors were brought to light and published.

So far, you will see, there was little which could be censured; the revival of learning was in itself a great benefit to mankind, and the labour which it involved was well bestowed. But, in this world, evil follows good as its shadow; human nature perverting and corrupting what is intrinsically innocent or praiseworthy. So, in this instance, the pursuit of the old learning became a passion. As the crumbling cloisters of the East were ransacked, and manuscripts were found and decyphered,—as the ruins of pagan edifices were excavated, mounds of earth removed, and the sculptures of classical art disinterred, an uncon-

* Nicholas V.

trollable excitement, an intoxication, seized upon the classes which were engaged in the work. It seized upon young and old: while one celebrated archeologist* spent fifty years in the discovery of ancient authors, and another's† hair turned white on his losing by shipwreck his cargo of discoveries, noble ladies became prodigies of learning, and a youth‡ of twenty exhibited himself at Rome as the master of twenty-two languages, and proposed nine hundred subjects for disputation.

The wonderful art of printing, which had been lately discovered, added to the excitement, not merely by what it actually did in that day, but by the brilliant future, which it opened on the imagination, to the advance both of knowledge and of society.

Nor was this the limit of the discoveries of that remarkable age;—news came of another continent beyond the ocean; America, North and South, became known to Europe, and the extent of the earth was doubled. The strangest tales were circulated, true and false, of the riches, of the gold, silver, and gems, of the animals, of the vegetable productions, of the new hemisphere.

* Poggio. † Guarino. ‡ Pico of Mirandola.

The public mind was agitated by a thousand fancies; no one knew what was coming; anything might be expected; a new era had opened upon the world, and enormous changes, political and social, were in preparation. There was an upheaving of the gigantic intellect of man; he found he had powers and resources which he was not conscious of before, and began in anticipation to idolize their triumphs.

And, while the world was becoming so strong, the Church, on the other hand, was at the moment proportionally weak, as far as relates to the human instruments of her power. Great, indeed, was her temporal exaltation at that day; great she was then, as she will ever be, in her invisible, divine strength; but in the ordinary elements of her greatness and weapons of her success, in order and discipline, in pastoral vigilance, in the sanctity of her individual members, in these respects certainly she was taken at disadvantage. I do not like, nor would you, my Brethren, wish me to enlarge upon a most sorrowful subject. The great Italian families intrigued and fought for her supreme rule, as if it had been a mere earthly principality. And, on this account, she was unable at the moment, from scarcity of champions, to cope with the vehement enthusiastic movement which I have been describing, and which assailed her within and without. All things are good in their place: human learning and science, the works of genius, the wonders of nature, all, as I have said, have their use, when kept in subordination to the faith and worship of God; but it is nothing else but an abuse, if they are suffered to engross the mind, and if religion is made secondary to them. Yet they are so fascinating,—so enchanting,—so present, tangible, constraining, in their influence,—that, unless the watchmen of the Holy City are on the alert, they are almost sure to act to the prejudice of the highest interests of man. So it was at the time I speak of; what was beautiful was placed before what was true; or rather, the beauty of the creature was preferred to the transcendent beauty of the Creator. Nature and art, the rich material, the creative mind, were suffered to invade and oppress the Church, instead of ministering to her. The world entered her sacred precincts forcibly, and embellished them after its own fashion. It addressed itself to her rulers, who were already enervated by the homage of nations; and it attempted to persuade them to disguise the awful Bride of the Lamb in an old heathen garb, of which her very coming had long since been the destruction. More seemly by far had it been to ask her to take part in the abolished ceremonies of the Mosaic law, than to intrude classical literature upon her instead of the teaching of the Holy Fathers. It was Satan carrying her up to the high mountain, and showing her all the kingdoms of the earth and their glory, with the hope of tempting her to forget her mission.

"Eat and drink, for to-morrow we die": so was it said of old by the heathen; so was it now said, almost in the same words, by Christians, not meaning, indeed, to deny the life to come, but hoping to inherit the future without giving up any enjoyment of the present. The artists, poets, and philosophers, who flourished under the smile of the great Florentine family, and their disciples through Italy, if they were not allowed to decorate Holy Church at their will and pleasure, at least could do as they would with the world; and fallen as it is, they made it still, by the splendour of their genius, a very paradise of delight. They flung a grace over sin, and a dignity over unbelief. Life was to them one long revel; they feasted, they sported, they moulded forms and painted countenances of the most perfect human beauty; they indulged in licentious wit, they wrote immodest verses, they lightly used the words of Scripture; they quarrelled, they used the knife, they fled to sanctuary, and then they issued forth again, to go through the same round of pleasure and of sin. Festivals and Carnivals became seasons of popular licence, for dramas and masquerades; and the excesses of paganism were renewed with the refinements supplied by classical associations. Dances, processions, and songs, formed part of the entertainment. Florence especially was the scene of the pageant, and its whole population were either actors in it, or spectators. The time chosen for it was the night; the performances were carried on by torchlight; bands of women, as well as of men, had their appointed parts in them, nor were they concluded till after daybreak. On St. John Baptist's day, in the year preceding St. Philip's birth, such an exhibition, with tournaments and other celebrations, was held in that same city, his birth-place. Seven sacred princes came up incognito to attend it; two lions and a panther were sent as a present from a member of the reigning family, then seated in the Vatican; and a triumphal arch was erected, in honour of the donor, opposite to the Dominican convent of St. Mark.

All this for the people:—Their rulers, who had introduced or patronized these shows, and the immediate circle of those rulers, went further. They took heathen names; they kept the feasts of the heathen founder of Rome, and the heathen philosopher Plato; they died with heathen consolations sounding in their ears. They attempted to hold intercourse with the evil powers;—we have the record of a scene in the great Roman amphitheatre, called the Coliseum. The sorcerer is said to have possessed a sacred character; thousands of devils are described as rising at his incantation, who promised, and who kept their promise, to grant a wicked gratification to the celebrated artist[*] who consulted them. A greater sin could not have been committed by an ecclesiastic, but scandals there were worse. If even in the very opening of the Gospel, when faith was keenest and the heart purest, there was a Judas among the Apostles, and a Nicolas among the deacons, and a Simon Magus among the

[*] Cellini.

neophytes, we need not wonder, much as we may lament, that in the degenerate age I am speaking of, lapses should occur, far more numerous than those early ones, if not so great in enormity of crime. One of the most zealous restorers of the ancient learning, who has been already spoken of, was an ecclesiastic with a family;* one of the chief writers of licentious tales had on him both religious and episcopal obligations.† And a writer,‡ who is reckoned the vilest of his day, being patronized by one of the great Florentine family at Rome, was audacious enough to set his heart (unsuccessfully) on becoming a Cardinal of Holy Church.

Good and evil, sacred prerogatives and sinful hearts, were brought into close contact, marvellously and awfully. The Sovereign Pontiffs were familiarly dealt with, and then slandered behind their backs, by the profligate artists whom they had benefited. Holy men grew up and won their crowns, out of families on which history has set its note of shame. Two saints, contemporaries of St. Philip, will occur to you, my dear Fathers, as instances of this portent:—St. Francis Borgia, the third Father-General of the Society

* Poggio. † Bandello. ‡ Pietro Aretino.

of Jesus, bears a name, shameful in the history of Rome; St. Mary Magdalene of the Pazzi came of a Florentine stock infamous for a deed of combined sacrilege, bloodshed, and treachery perhaps without a parallel.

These are some of the traits of the times in which St. Philip was sent on earth; certainly, an Apostle was needed both for Florence and for Rome.

2. And for Florence, that Apostle seemed to have been found just before St. Philip's day. You may recollect, my Brethren, I have several times spoken of the great Dominican convent of St. Mark. That convent, built though it was by the first prince of the rich family I have so often mentioned, was devoted to a style of art and a description of learning far different from those for which Greece or Rome was famous. Under the shadow of St. Dominic, such learning alone had place, which ministered to the most symmetrical theology, and to a philosophy in accordance; and the serene wisdom, which his name recalls, had been carried out into poetry and the fine arts, by the genius of his children and his clients. That very convent of St. Mark is still

adorned by the celebrated paintings executed by the beatified Dominican artist, called, like St. Thomas, the Angelical; and about the same time, it had been under the rule of the celebrated Dominican confessor and writer, afterwards archbishop of the city, St. Antoninus. Here, too, came, about thirty years afterwards, and shortly before St. Philip's birth, that fiery Reformer, also a Dominican, of whom I am to speak as a sort of Apostle of Florence, a man certainly of commanding eloquence and extraordinary influence, full of the traditions of his order, and cherishing a fierce hatred of the reviving heathen literature and the classical taste of the day; I mention his name, on account of the affection which St. Philip felt for his memory,—Savonarola.

A true son of St. Dominic, in energy, in severity of life, in contempt of merely secular learning, a forerunner of St. Pius the Fifth in boldness, in resoluteness, in zeal for the honour of the House of God, and for the restoration of holy discipline, Savonarola felt "his spirit stirred up within him", like another Paul, when he came to that beautiful home of genius and philosophy; for he found Florence, like another Athens, "wholly given to idolatry". He groaned within him, and was troubled, and refused consolation, when he beheld a Christian court and people priding itself on its material greatness, its intellectual gifts, and its social refinement, while it abandoned itself to luxury, to feast and song and revel, to fine shows and splendid apparel, to an impure poetry, to a depraved and sensual character of art, to heathen speculations, and to forbidden, superstitious practices. His vehement spirit could not be restrained, and got the better of him, and,—unlike the Apostle, whose prudence, gentleness, love of his kind, and human accomplishments are nowhere more happily shown than in his speech to the Athenians,*—he burst forth into a whirlwind of indignation and invective against all that he found in Florence, and condemned the whole established system, and all who took part of it, high and low, prince or prelate, ecclesiastic or layman, with a pitiless rigour,—which for the moment certainly did a great deal more than St. Paul was able to do at the Areopagus; for St. Paul made only one or two converts there, and departed, whereas Savonarola had great immediate success, frightened and abashed the offenders,

* *Acts*, xvii.

rallied round him the better disposed, and elicited and developed whatever there was of piety, whether in the multitude or in the upper class.

It was the truth of his cause, the earnestness of his convictions, the singleness of his aims, the impartiality of his censures, the intrepidity of his menaces, which constituted the secret of his success. Yet a less worthy motive lent its aid; men crowded round a pulpit, from which others were attacked as well as themselves. The humble offender was pleased to be told that crime was a leveller of ranks, and to find that he thus was a gainer in the common demoralization. The laity bore to be denounced, when the clergy were not spared; and the rich and noble suffered a declamation which did not stop short of the sacred Chair of St. Peter.

"In the houses of great prelates and great doctors", he cried out, "nothing is thought of but poetry and rhetoric. Go and see for yourselves: you will find them with books of polite literature in their hands, pernicious writings, with Virgil, Horace, and Cicero, to prepare themselves for the cure of souls withal. Astrologers have the governance of the Church. There is not a prelate, there is not a great doctor, but is intimate with some astrologer, who predicts for him the hour and the moment for riding out, or for whatever else he does. Our preachers have already given up Holy Scripture, and are given to philosophy, which they preach from the pulpit, and make it their queen. As to Holy Scripture, they treat it as the handmaid, because to preach philosophy looks learned, whereas it should simply be an aid in the interpretation of the divine word".

"Our Church", he continued, "has outside many fine ceremonies in divine worship, fine vestments, an uncommon display of drapery, gold and silver candlesticks, so many fine chalices, quite magnificent. Those great prelates with their fine mitres on, of gold and jewels, with crosiers of silver, with their fine chasubles, and copes of brocade, there they are at the altar, singing fine vespers, fine masses, so solemnly, with so many fine ceremonies, so many organs and singers, that your head turns. And they seem to you, those men, to have great gravity and a saintly show; and you think that they cannot do wrong, but that their words and their deeds are Gospel, and claim your observance.

That is how the modern Church is made. Men feed on these husks, and make themselves happy in these ceremonies, and say that the Church of Jesus Christ never was in a more flourishing state, and that divine worship never was so well carried out as at present,—as on one occasion a great prelate said, that the Church never was in such honour, and its prelates never in such repute, whereas its first prelates were but small men, because they were humble and poor, because they had not such ample bishoprics, such rich abbeys, as ours of this day, nor had they as yet such gold mitres, such chalices. Do you take me? I mean in the primitive Church, the chalices were of wood, and the prelates of gold; but now the chalices are of gold, and the prelates are wooden".

" O Italy !" he cried out in the tone of a prophet, " O rulers of Italy ! O prelates of the Church ! the wrath of God is over you, and your conversion alone will avert it. Do penance, while the sword is in the scabbard, and ere it is imbrued in your blood. O Italy ! thou shalt be given into the hands of a fierce, a barbarous nation, whose only pleasure will be to do thee ill. And Rome shall fare worse from them than any other city; your possessions and your treasures shall be given into their hands".

Such bold language effected for the moment a revolution rather than a reform. The eloquent preacher became the political partizan; the great family was forced by political circumstances to give way, and for the better part of ten years Savonarola was ruler of Florence. Not only the populace, but courtiers, noble ladies, scholars, artists, all put themselves at his disposal, and became his disciples. He found a way to the hearts of philosophers, poets, painters, engravers, sculptors, architects, and made them renounce their heathen tastes and heathen aspirations. "Behold the sun", he said; "its beauty consists in possessing light; behold the blessed spirits, their beauty is light; and God Himself, because He is the most full of light, is beauty itself. The beauty of every creature is more perfect, the more closely it resembles God's beauty; and the body is beautiful in proportion to the beauty of the soul. Conceive what must have been the beauty of the Blessed Virgin, who possessed such sanctity, sanctity that shone from all her features. Conceive how beautiful was Christ, who was God and man. Now even Aristotle, who was a pagan, bids us not to tolerate indecent pictures, lest children, seeing them, be corrupted; but what shall I say to you, Christian painters, who execute these immodest figures? I tell you to do so no more. You who have them and destroy them, will do a work pleasing to Almighty God and the Holy Virgin. 'You have dedicated My Temple and My Churches to your God Moloch', says the Almighty. See how they act at Florence! mothers take their married daughters to the cathedral, decked out for show, till they look like nymphs. 'These are your idols, which you have placed in My Temple'. The young men say of this or that maiden, 'This is Magdalen', 'That is St. John', because you paint figures in the church, which resemble this woman or that. You painters act wrongly; you introduce worldly vanities into the Church. Do you believe that the Blessed Virgin was dressed as you represent her? I tell you that she was modestly dressed, and so veiled that one could scarce see her face; and St. Elizabeth too was modest and simple in her attire".*

Wonderful were the conversions which followed on the enunciation of truth, so undeniable,

* *Vide* Father Meehan's translation of Marchetti's work.

so grave in import, so earnestly enforced. As to the artists, many of them became Dominicans, and the convent of St. Mark had to be enlarged to hold them. The members of another convent in the city, feeling their state of relaxation, begged to be allowed to come over to him in a body, and to take the rule of St. Dominic upon them. The population of Florence rose from their beds after midnight in winter to attend upon his sermons. There they stood in the Church, waiting, taper in hand, or singing hymns, or praying, or saying office, for three or four hours, till he began to preach. They showed the fruits of his exhortations in their homes. Women reformed their dress, youths unlearned their light songs, heads of families read the lives of the Saints to their children. At length the zealous preacher determined on having, in token of repentance, a solemn conflagration in the great square, of all the scandals and the various occasions of sin with which the city abounded. At the time of the Carnival, the special festival of the world, the flesh, and the devil, he invited the whole city to this stern act of reparation. He raised a high pyramid, with a quantity of gunpowder at its base. His innumerable penitents formed in long procession, and hither they marched with the instruments and incentives of iniquity in their hands, to be offered up in expiation of their sins. It was a costly sacrifice, ruthlessly performed. Artists brought their beautiful pictures, portraits, and figures, in ivory or alabaster, and flung them upon the pyre; others brought richly-worked tapestries; others, lutes, flutes, guitars, cards, dice, looking-glasses, perfumery, paint, masks, disguises; others, novels and poems. Lighted torches were then applied, and, amid the ringing of bells and the acclamations of the vast multitude, the whole was reduced to ashes. A foreigner had in vain offered 20,000 crowns to ransom them from the flames. The same impressive ceremony was repeated in the following year.

A very wonderful man, you will allow, my Brethren, was this Savonarola. I shall say nothing more of him, except what was the issue of his reforms. For years, as I have said, he had his own way; at length, his innocence, sincerity, and zeal were too much for his humility. He presumed; he exalted himself against a power which none can assail without misfortune. He put himself in opposition to the Holy

See, and, as some say, disobeyed its injunctions. Reform is not wrought out by disobedience; this was not the way to be the Apostle either of Florence or of Rome. Then trouble came upon him, a great reaction ensued; his enemies got the upper hand; he went into extravagances himself; the people deserted him; he was put to death, strangled, hung on a gibbet, and then burned in the very square where he had set fire to the costly furniture of vanity and sin. And then the rich and powerful family returned to Florence; and things went on pretty much as before; and, the very year preceding St. Philip's birth, took place that riotous festivity on St. John Baptist's day, over against the convent of St. Mark, of which I have already spoken.

And now I have added something more to the picture, which I have proposed to give you, of the state of things both in Florence and in Rome, when St. Philip was raised up to be an Apostle of another sort.

PART II.

FLORENCE, then, had her Apostle;—we have reviewed his commencement and his end:—a zealous, heroic man, but not, as far as we can judge, reaching to the level of a saint. It is not by the enthusiasm of the multitude, or by political violence,—it is not by powerful declamation, or by railing at authorities, that the foundations are laid of religious works. It is not by sudden popularity, or by strong resolves and demonstrations, or by romantic incidents, or by immediate successes, that undertakings commence which are to last. I do not say, that to be roused, even for a moment, from the dream of sin, to repent and be absolved, even though a relapse follow, is a slight gain; or that the brilliant, but brief, triumphs of Savonarola are to be despised. He did good in his day, though his day was a short one. Still, after all, his history brings to mind that passage in sacred history, where the Almighty displayed His presence to Elias on Mount Horeb. "The Lord was not in the wind", nor "in the earthquake", nor "in the fire"; but after the fire came "the whisper of a gentle air".

So was it with the Lord of grace Himself, when He came upon earth; so it is with His chosen servants after Him. He grew up in silence and obscurity, overlooked by the world; and then He triumphed. He was the grain cast into the earth, which, while a man sleeps and rises, night and day, springs up and grows whilst he knoweth not. He was the mustard seed, "which is the least of all seeds, but, when it is grown up, becometh a tree, and shooteth out great branches, so that the birds of the air dwell under its shadow". He grew up "as a tender plant, and as a root out of a thirsty land"; and "His look was, as it were, hidden and despised, wherefore we esteemed Him not". And, when He began to preach, He did not "contend nor cry out, nor break the bruised reed, nor quench the smoking flax"; and thus "He sent forth judgment unto victory". So was it in the beginning, so has it been ever since. After the earthquake and the fire, the calm, soothing whisper of the fragrant air. After Savonarola, Philip.

1. Philip was born in Florence within twenty years after him. The memory of the heroic friar

was then still fresh in the minds of men, who would be talking familiarly of him to the younger generation,—of the scenes which their own eyes had witnessed, and of the deeds of penance which they had done at his bidding. Especially vivid would the recollections of him be in the Convent of St. Mark; for there was his cell, there the garden where he walked up and down in meditation, and refused to notice the great prince of the day;* there would be his crucifix, his habit, his discipline, his books, and whatever had once been his. Now, it so happened, St.. Philip was a child of this very convent; here he received his first religious instruction, and in after times he used to say, " Whatever there was of good in me, when I was young, I owed it to the Fathers of St. Mark's, in Florence". For Savonarola he retained a singular affection all through his life; he kept his picture in his room, and about the year 1560, when the question came before Popes Paul IV. and Pius IV., of the condemnation of Savonarola's teaching, he interceded fervently and successfully in his behalf before the Blessed Sacrament, exposed on the oc-

* Lorenzo de' Medici.

casion in the Dominican church at Rome. This was in his middle age.

To return to his youth: at the age of eighteen, he left Florence for good, first going to a town in the kingdom of Naples; then, at the end of two years, to Rome, where he lived for sixty years, without once going beyond the circuit of its seven Basilicas. There he died, when he had nearly completed his eightieth year. A simple outline of a history, you will say, my Brethren, singularly deficient in incident or adventure; yet, though he made only one journey in his long life, he turned it to account; and the changes of external situation which then befell him, few as they were, were instruments in the formation of his mind and direction of his future course. The Florentine pupil of St. Dominic fell under the inspirations of St. Benedict in the territory of Naples, and found St. Ignatius in person and in the flesh, when he got to Rome.

Benedict, Dominic, Ignatius:—these are the three venerable Patriarchs, whose Orders divide between them the extent of Christian history. There are many Saints besides, who have been fruitful in followers and institutions, and have multiplied themselves in Christendom, and lived on earth in their children, when they themselves were gone to heaven. But there are three who, in an especial way, have had committed to them the office of a public ministry in the affairs of the Church one after another, and who are, in some sense, her "nursing fathers", and are masters in the spiritual Israel, and ruling names in her schools and her libraries; and these are Benedict, Dominic, and Ignatius. Philip came under the teaching of all three successively.

2. It was the magnificent aim of the children of St. Dominic to form the whole matter of human knowledge into one harmonious system, to secure the alliance between religion and philosophy, and to train men to the use of the gifts of nature in the sunlight of divine grace and revealed truth. It required the dissolution and reconstruction of society to give an opportunity for so great a thought; and accordingly, the Order of Preachers flourished after the old Empire had passed away, and the chaos which followed on it had resulted in the creation of a new world. Now, in the age of St. Philip, a violent effort was in progress, on the part of the powers of evil, to break up this sublime unity, and to set human genius, the philosopher and the poet, the

artist and the musician, in opposition to religion. Accordingly, the work of the glorious Order of St. Dominic was more than ever called for, whatever might be those new methods of prosecuting it, more suitable to the times; and, if Philip was destined, as he was, to play an important part in them in the cause of God, it was therefore necessary that he should be imbued with the great idea of that Order. It was necessary that he should have deeply fixed within him, as the object of his life, that single aim of subduing this various, multiform, many-coloured world to the unity of divine service. I mean, there are Saints, whose mission lies rather in separating off from each other the world and the Truth; that of other Saints lies in bringing them together. Philip's was the latter. Suitably then, and reasonably, did he receive his elementary formation of mind from the Fathers of St. Mark. And when this had been secured, then he was sent off, "not knowing whither he went", to other tutors, and towards the scene of his destined labours, to do a work like St. Dominic's work, though he was not to be a Dominican.

3. Then he came to St. Benedict. Close by

the town, to which his father had sent him, is the celebrated monastery of Monte Cassino, the principal seat of the Benedictine Order. The relaxation, which at that time prevailed in so many regular communities, seems not to have reached this ancient sanctuary;* but the judgments, which even in Savonarola's day were falling on Italy, had not fallen short of Monte Cassino. The neighbourhood had been the scene of war; and the foreign troops had pillaged the Church, and the new generation of monks had been nurtured in adversity. "Not far from San Germano", that is, the town to which Philip had been sent, says the author of his life, "there is a celebrated mountain, which, according to a very ancient and common tradition, is one of those which opened at our Saviour's death. It belongs to the Benedictine Fathers of Monte Cassino, who have a church there dedicated to the Most Holy Trinity. This mountain is split from top to bottom by three huge fissures; and in the middle of the three, which is the steepest, there is a little chapel on a rock, under the care of the monks, and on it is a crucifix painted, which the sailors

* *Vide* Tosti's history of that abbey.

salute with their guns, as they pass under. Here Philip was in the habit of retiring for prayer and meditation on the Lord's Passion".

Observe, my dear Brethren, Philip is now in quite a new scene,—no longer amid the medieval grandeur, but among the Saints and associations of primitive ages; it is no longer the busy, gaudy town, but the calm and pure country; no longer cloisters and paintings, but rocks and sea, leading to meditation; no longer golden mitres and jewelled copes, under high arches and painted windows, but secluded, unfurnished chapels, and rude crucifixes; no longer the vision of our Lord's Passion pourtrayed by sacred art, but the very rent in the solid mountain, opened in that same hour when He hung upon the Cross; no longer the holy doctrines and devotions of later piety, but the aboriginal mystery, contained in Scripture, Creed, and Baptism, and battled for in the first centuries, the dogma of the Most Holy Trinity. Thus, everything about Philip threw him back into the times of simplicity, of poverty, of persecution, of martyrdom; the times of patience, of obscure and cheerful toil, of humble, unrequited service; ere Christianity had gained a literature, or theology had become a science, or any but saints had sat in Peter's chair; while the book of nature and the book of grace were the chief instruments of knowledge and of love. Such was the school of St. Benedict; nor did that dear and venerable Father let the young pilgrim go, even when his two years' sojourn in his neighbourhood was at an end. For if a direct divine summons took him to Rome, still St. Benedict, as I may say, chose out for him his lodging there; for he sent him to those ancient basilicas, and cemeteries, and catacombs of the Holy City, which spoke of the early monks and the primitive religion, and these you know he haunted, or almost lived in them, till ten years and more had passed from the date of his leaving Florence. "Philip Neri is a great saint", said a Dominican Friar, who kept his eyes upon the youth; "and among his other wonderful things, he has dwelt for a whole ten years in the caves of St. Sebastian, by way of penance"; lodging, I say, as St. Benedict would have had him, with the old martyr Popes, and their saintly court and retinue, their deacons and chamberlains, and chaplains; with St. Callistus, and St. Sebastian, and St. Laurence; with St. Mark and St. Marcellian, with St. Agnes and St. Cecilia, with St. Nereus and St. Achilleus, with

St. Papias, and St. Maurus, till at length he had that marvellous visitation, when the Holy Ghost came down upon him in a ball of fire, about the time of Pentecost, and filled his heart with consolations so overwhelming that, lest he should die of ecstasy, he came up into the world of men, and set about a work to flesh and blood more endurable.

Thus was the second stage of Philip's education brought to a close; and, as from St. Dominic he gained the end he was to pursue, so from St. Benedict he learned how to pursue it. He was to pursue Savonarola's purposes, but not in Savonarola's way; rather, in the spirit and after the fashion of those early Religious, of which St. Benedict is the typical representative. Those early Religious lived in communities, which were detached from each other, not brought together under one common governance; they were settled in one place, and had no duties beyond it; vows were not a necessary element of their state; they had little or nothing to do with ecclesiastical matters or secular politics; they had no large plan of action for religious ends; they let each day do its work as it came; they lived in obscurity, and laid a special stress on prayer and meditation; they were simple in their forms of worship, and they freely admitted laymen into their fellowship. In peculiarities such as these we recognize the Oratory of St. Philip. Least thought had he of all men, of living in his works beyond his day: he could scarcely be brought to throw his disciples into the form of community, and to perpetuate it by ecclesiastical recognition. Then he would not go and preside over them; then, when obliged to go, he would not let them call him Father Superior. Then he would not listen to their founding houses in other cities. Much less would he take dignities himself, or suffer them to do so. He would not permit any forms or observances to be the characteristics of his congregation, besides mutual love and hard work. For the interior life he sent them back, with especial earnestness, to the Apostolic Epistles, and to the traditions of that early monk, John Cassian. In his exterior worship, he imitated, as Cardinal Baronius observes, the form furnished by St. Paul, in his first Epistle to the Corinthians. "It is by a divine counsel", says that glory of the Oratory, speaking, in his Annals, in the tone of an historian, "that there has been in great measure renewed in our age in

Rome, after the pattern of the Apostolic assembly, the edifying practice of discoursing in sermons of the things of God. This has been the work of the Reverend Father Philip Neri, a Florentine, who, like a skilful architect, laid the foundation of it. It was arranged, that almost every day those who were desirous of Christian perfection should come to the Oratory. First, there was some length of time spent in mental prayer, then one of the brothers read a spiritual book, and during the reading the aforesaid Father commented on what was read. Sometimes he desired one of the brethren to give his opinion on some subject, and then the discourse proceeded in the form of dialogue. After this, he commanded one of them to mount a seat, and there, in a familiar, plain style, to discourse upon the lives of the Saints. To him succeeded another, on a different subject, but equally plain; lastly, a third discoursed upon ecclesiastical history. When all was finished, they sang some spiritual hymn, prayed again for a short time, and so ended. Things being thus disposed, and approved by the Pope's authority, it seemed as though the beautiful form of the Apostolical assembly had returned, as far as times admitted".

This, of course, took place long after that portion of Philip's life, on which I am immediately engaged. From eight to eighteen, ten years, he was under the teaching of St. Dominic; from eighteen to twenty-eight or twenty-nine, he was with St. Benedict, and the ancient Saints of Rome. Nor even, when the end of that period was come, did he quite leave St. Benedict. During the whole sixty years that he passed at Rome, there was only one great turning-point or crisis of his life; it was when, at about the age of forty, he thought of going to the East. Now, to determine this point, he did not take the counsel of any Dominican, nor of any Jesuit, either of which courses might have seemed natural, but he went to a Benedictine of the great Basilica of St. Paul, and by him was referred to another monk of the Benedictine family, who lived on the spot of St. Paul's martyrdom; and this father, directed by St. John the Evangelist, told him that "*his* Indies were to be in Rome, where God would make much use of him". Observe this, too, my Brethren: St. John the Evangelist was the informant. Philip lives in especial intercourse with the Saints of the Apostolic ages, with St. Paul, with St. John the Evangelist. Again, St. Mary

Magdalen and St. Philip and St. James were his own particular patrons; and St. John the Baptist appeared to him in vision. I do not recollect any Saints of a later date, with whom he was in such intimate communion.

4. Such was the character of the devotions, such the cast and fashion of interior life, which are proper to St. Philip; Benedictine, as I may call them. At length he came back to the world, and there he found and made acquaintance with the third great Patriarch, whom I have named, St. Ignatius, who was then in Rome. That memorable Saint had taken up his abode, and established his Society there, while Philip was in his long retreat, and now he was at hand for Philip to hear and to consult, for the space of eleven years, when he died. Now what did St. Ignatius do for him? There is a remarkable resemblance, as any one may see, in the practical teaching of the two, and that, in matters where that teaching is in contrast to what was more usual in and before their day. It cannot be doubted that, while in theological traditions St. Philip was one with St. Dominic, in the cure of souls he was one with St. Ignatius. An earnest

THE MISSION OF ST. PHILIP. 311

enforcement of interior religion, a jealousy of formal ceremonies, an insisting on obedience rather than sacrifice, on mental discipline rather than fasting or hair-shirt, a mortification of the reason, that illumination and freedom of spirit which comes of love; further, a mild and tender rule for the confessional; frequent confessions, frequent communions, special devotion towards the Blessed Sacrament, these are peculiarities of a particular school in the Church, and St. Ignatius and St. Philip are Masters in it. From St. Benedict's time there had been a broad line between the world and the Church, and it was very hard to follow sanctity without entering into Religion. St. Ignatius and St. Philip, on the contrary, carried out the Church into the world, and aimed to bring under her light yoke as many men as they could possibly reach. Both of them, of course, acted under a divine guidance; but, as they lived at the same time and on the same spot, it is natural to think that, humanly speaking, one must have taken his tradition from the other; and, as St. Philip is the younger, it is as natural to think that he gained it from St. Ignatius. As then he learned from

Benedict *what to be*, and from Dominic *what to do*, so let me consider that from Ignatius he learned *how he was to do it*.

St. Philip, on one occasion, acknowledged his debt in one particular to the older Saint; he said to some Jesuits whom he met, " You are children of a great Father. I am under obligations to him, for your Master, Ignatius, taught me to make mental prayer". Nay, strange as it may appear, it would seem that, at least at one time of his life, he wished to be admitted among his children; at another time, perhaps, to which I have already alluded, to join them in the East with others in his company.

5. My Brethren, I do not feel it to be any want of devotion or reverence towards our dear Father, to speak of him as looking out to be taught, or willing to be governed. It is like his most amiable, natural, and unpretending self. He was ever putting himself in the back ground, and never thought of taking on himself rule, or seizing on a position, in the Church, or of founding a religious body. And I seem to have Father Consolini's authority for saying that I please him more by doing towards him what he would do for himself, than by showing now a zeal in his

behalf, for which he would not have thanked me when living. Father Consolini, as you recollect, was the most intimate friend of St. Philip, of all his spiritual children. The Saint "was most jealous in concealing his gifts from the eyes of the world", but "from Consolini he hid nothing". Well, then, you would think, that after Philip's death, his loving disciple would tell all that he could, as loudly and as widely as he could, in his honour. Not so; so far from it, that the author of that Father's life, whom I have just been quoting, tells us that, although he was the most devoted, as well as the best beloved of the sons of St. Philip, yet, when the Holy Father's canonization was first commenced, he did not wish it to be forwarded by the Congregation. He himself at first refused to give evidence in the Process, and, when commanded by his Superiors, he gave it with evident reluctance. How natural this is! St. Philip was too *near* him to allow of his speaking to his praise. To praise him was to praise himself and all the Fathers. Let strangers praise him, not a son of his own. And if they wish to love him, let them come and learn to love him for what he is. We do not wish him other than he is; we love him too much for what he is, to wish him praised for what he is not.

It is further said of Father Consolini: " He was so deeply penetrated with this feeling, that, though he knew from the Saint himself the way in which he received from the Holy Ghost that wonderful visitation of the fracture of his ribs, yet he never revealed the particulars to any living person till within a few days of his death". He recollected the Saint's words, "*Secretum meum mihi*", "My secret is my own". And again: "When he heard that some priests had united together under the invocation and institute of St. Philip, with the name of Reformed Priests, he was gravely displeased with the vanity of such a title, saying, that had Philip been living, he would have gone to the Pope to dissolve such a congregation".

O touching and most genuine traits of our sweetest and dearest Father, and most impressive lesson to us, and remarkable contrast to the spirit of the vehement friar of St. Mark's! Philip had shown them from a boy. One of the first things told us of him in his very childhood is, that "he never spoke lightly, as boys do, of becoming a priest or a religious; he concealed the wish of his heart, and from chilhood upwards he eschewed display, of which he ever had a special hatred". Things which other saints have allowed in themselves, or rather have felt a duty, he could not abide. He did not ask to be opposed, to be maligned, to be persecuted, but simply to be overlooked, to be despised. Neglect was the badge which he desired for himself and for his own. " To despise the whole world", he said, " to despise no member of it, to despise oneself, *to despise being despised"*. He took great pleasure in being undervalued and made little of, according to the Apostle's sentiment, " If any man among you seem to be wise, let him become a fool, that he may be wise". And hence you know, when he became so famous in his old age, and every one was thinking of him mysteriously, and looking at him with awe, and solemnly repeating Father Philip's words and rehearsing Father Philip's deeds, and bringing strangers to see him, it was the most cruel of penances to him, and he was ever behaving himself ridiculously on purpose, and putting them out, from his intense hatred and impatience of being turned into a show. "He was always trying", says his biographer, " either by gestures, or motions, or words, or some facetious levity, to hide his great devotion; and when he had done any virtuous action, he would do something simple to cover it".

6. This being the disposition of St. Philip, you will understand how it was, that while he wished to do the very work which Savonarola intended, he set about it, not on principle merely, but on instinctive feeling, in so different a way. Here, as in other cases, the slowest way was the surest, and the most quiet the most effectual; and he rather would not have attempted that work at all, than have sacrificed his humility and modesty to the doing of it. Accordingly he, whose mission was to Popes, Cardinals, and nobles, to philosophers, authors, and artists, began with teaching the poor who are found about the doors of the Roman churches. This was his occupation for years; soon he added to it another undertaking of the same kind. He used to go about the squares,* shops, warehouses, schools, and shop-counters, "talking with all sorts of persons in a most engaging way about spiritual things, and saying, ' Well, my brothers, when are we to set about serving God, and doing good?'" and he began to make some great conversions.

Rome was at that time in a very different state from what it was when Savonarola had discharged his threats upon it. A most heavy judgment had come upon it a few years before Philip arrived there, and that judgment had come in mercy upon the city of God's choice. The Germans and Spaniards had besieged, taken, and sacked it, with excesses and outrages so horrible, that it is thought to have suffered less from the Goths and Huns than from troops nominally Christian. Its external splendour has never been recovered down to this day; its churches were spoiled and defaced; its convents plundered; its Cardinals, Bishops, monks, and nuns, treated with the most extreme indignities, and many of them murdered; and sacrileges committed innumerable. People thought what happened was the fulfilment of the predictions of Savonarola; but, amid these miseries, the grace of God spoke, and the guilty population was softened. First St. Caietan, who was himself tortured by the ruffianly soldiers, had already begun to call to prayer and repentance; St. Ignatius followed, preaching. Then came St. Philip, but in his own quiet way, like " the whispering of a gentle air", " his speech trickling like dew, as a shower upon the herb, and as drops upon the grass".

He began, as I have said, with the poor; then he went among shopmen, warehousemen, clerks in banks, and loungers in public places. Encouraged by these successes, he addressed himself to men, not merely of careless, but of the worst kind of lives, and them also he gained for God. His charity brought him into various situations of trial; but when attempts were made upon his virtue, his zeal and devotion brought him through them. All this time he was visiting the hospitals, and attending to the necessities, both bodily and spiritual, of the sick.

This had been his life, in some degree, before he left his retreat in the basilicas and cemeteries; and it lasted altogether ten years. At the end of them he joined a small community of pious people, in number fifteen, "simple and poor", we are told, "but full of spirit and devotion", and "inflaming one another, by words and by example, with the desire of Christian perfection". Philip, though still a layman, preached: and, because he was doing an unusual thing, dissolute youths came to make game of him; but it was dangerous for such to come near him: on one occasion he converted thirty of them by a single sermon. He and his associates made it their duty to attend on the pilgrims, and on the sick who had left the hospitals, convalescent, but not recovered. Thus his work gradually extended; for these pilgrims and sick were from all countries, and many of them were Jews or heretics, whom he brought into the fold of the Church.

7. He had been fifteen years in Rome before he was ordained; and then at length, on his receiving faculties for hearing confessions, he began, at the age of thirty-five, his real mission,—that long course of ministry, which, carried on for years three times fifteen, down almost to the hour of his death, has gained for him the title of Apostle of Rome.

You know, my Brethren, what is commonly meant by an Apostle of a country. It means one who converts its heathen inhabitants to the Christian faith, such as St. Augustine of England; accordingly, his proper function is Baptism. Hence, you find St. Augustine, St. Patrick, St. Boniface, or St. Francis baptizing their hundreds and thousands. This was the office to which St. Philip wished to minister in India; but it was his zeal and charity that urged him, not his mature judgment; for the fierce conflicts, and the pastoral cares, and the rude publicity of such exalted duties, were unsuited to his nature; so he was kept at home for a different work. He was kept at home, in the very heart of Christendom, not to evangelize, but to recover; and his instrument of conversion was, not Baptism, but Penance. The Confessional was the seat and seal of his peculiar Apostolate. Hence, as St. Francis Xavier baptized his tens of thousands, Philip was, every day and almost every hour, for forty-five years, restoring, teaching, encouraging, and guiding penitents along the narrow way of salvation.

We are told in his Life, that "he abandoned every other care, and gave himself to hearing confessions". Not content with the day, he gave up a considerable portion of the night to it also. Before dawn he had generally confessed a good number. When he retired to his room, he still confessed every one who came; though at prayers, though at meals, he broke off instantly, and attended to the call. When the church was opened at daybreak, he went down to the Confessional, and remained in it till noon, when he said Mass. When no penitents came, he remained near his Confessional; he never intermitted hearing confessions for any illness. " On the day of his death, he began to hear confessions very early in the morning"; after Mass "again he went into the Confessional"; in the afternoon, and " during the rest of the day down to supper time", he heard confessions. After supper, " he heard the confessions of those Fathers who were to say the first Masses on the following morning", when he himself was no longer to be on earth. It was this extraordinary persevering service in so trying, so wearing a duty, for forty-five years, that enabled him to be the new Apostle of the Sacred City. Thus it was, as the lesson in his Office says, that " he bore innumerable children to Christ". He was ever suffering their miseries, and fighting with their sins, and travailing with their good resolves, year after year, whatever their state of life, their calling, their circumstances, if so be that he might bring them safe to heaven, with a superhuman, heroic patience, of which we see so few traces in the fiery preacher at Florence.

Savonarola, in spite of his personal sanctity, in spite of his protests against a mere external sanctity in the Church, after all, began with an external reform; he burned lutes and guitars, looking-glasses and masks, books and pictures, in the public square: but Philip bore with every outside extravagance in those whom he addressed, as far as it was not directly sinful, knowing well that if the heart was once set right, the appropriate demeanour would follow. You recollect how a youth came to his Exercises one day, dressed out "in a most singular and whimsical fashion"; and how Philip did but fix his eyes on him, and proceed with the discourses and devotions of the Oratory, and how, by the time, that they were at an end, the poor sinner had become quite another man; his nature was changed all at once, and he became one of the Saint's most fervent penitents. A rich ecclesiastic came to him in coloured clothes, like a layman: Philip talked with him for a fortnight, without saying a word about his dress. At the end of the time he put it off of his own accord, and made a general confession. His biographer says: " He was very much against stiffness and offhand prohibitions about wearing fine clothes, collars, swords, and such like things, saying that if only a little devotion gained admittance into their hearts, you might leave them to themselves. If he spoke of them, it was good-naturedly and playfully. You recollect he said to a lady, who asked if it was a sin to wear slippers with very high heels, according to an excessive fashion of the day; 'Take care they do not trip you up'. And to a youth, who wore one of those large, stiff frills, which we see in pictures, he remarked, ' I should caress you much more, if your collar did not hurt me' ".

Savonarola is associated in our minds with the pulpit rather than the confessional: his vehemence converted many, but frightened or irritated more. The consequences came back upon himself and his penitents. Some of his convert artists were assassinated, others were driven into exile, others gave up their profession altogether in disgust or despair. Philip had no vocation, and little affection, for the pulpit; he was jealous of what the world calls eloquence, and he mortified his disciples when they aspired to it. One he interrupted and sent down; another he made preach his sermon six times over: he discoursed and conversed rather than preached. And "he could not endure harsh rebukes", says the writer of his life, "or anything like rigour. He allured men to the service of God so dexterously, and with such a holy, winning art, that those who saw it cried out, astonished: 'Father Philip draws souls as the magnet draws iron'. He so accommodated himself to the temper of each, as, in the words of the Apostle, to become 'all things to all men, that he might gain all'". And his love of them individually was so tender and ardent, that, even in extreme old age, he was anxious to suffer for their sins; and "for this end he inflicted on himself severe disciplines, and he reckoned their misdeeds as his own, and wept for them as such". I do not read that Savonarola acted thus towards Pope Alexander the Sixth, whom he so violently denounced.

It is not surprising that, with this tenderness, with this prudence, and with the zeal and charity to which both were subordinate, his influence increased year by year, till he gained a place in the heart of the Roman population, which he has never lost. There are those whose greatest works are their earliest; there are others, who, at first scarcely distinguishable from a whole class who look the same, distance them in the long run, and do more and more wonderful works the longer they live. Philip was thirty-five before he was ordained; forty, before he began his exercises in his room; fifty, before he had a church; sixty, before he formed his disciples into a congregation; near seventy, before he put himself at the head of it. As the Blessed Virgin's Name has by a majestic growth expanded and extended itself through the Church, " taking root in an honourable people, and resting in the Holy City", so the influence of Philip was, at the end of many years, paramount in that place which he had so long dwelt in as an obscure, disregarded stranger. Sharp eyes and holy sympathies indeed had detected "Philip Neri, as a saint living in caves", when he was a youth; but it required half a century to develop this truth to the intelligence of the multitude of men. At length there was no possibility of mistaking it. Visitors to Rome discerned the presence of one who was greater than pope and cardinals, holy, venerable, and vigilant as the rulers of the Church then were. " Among all the wonderful things which I saw in Rome", says one of them, writing when Philip was turned fifty, " I took the chief pleasure in beholding the multitude of devout and spiritual persons who frequented the Oratory. Amid the monuments of antiquity, the superb palaces and courts of so many illustrious lords, it appeared to me that the glory of this exemplar shone forth with surpassing light". "I go", says another visitor, ten years later, "to the Oratory, where they deliver every day most beautiful discourses on the gospel, or on the virtues and vices, or ecclesiastical history, or the lives of the saints. Persons of distinction go to hear them, bishops, prelates, and the like. They who deliver them are in holy orders, and of most exemplary life. Their superior is a certain Reverend Father Philip, an old man of sixty, who, they say, is an oracle, not only in Rome, but in the far off parts of Italy, and of France and Spain, so that many come to him for counsel; indeed he is another Thomas a Kempis, or Tauler".

But it required to live in Rome to understand what his influence really was. Nothing was too high for him, nothing too low. He taught poor begging women to use mental prayer; he took out boys to play; he protected orphans; he acted as novice-master to the children of St. Dominic. He was the teacher and director of artizans, mechanics, cashiers in banks, merchants, workers in gold, artists, men of science. He was consulted by monks, canons, lawyers, physicians, courtiers; ladies of the highest rank, convicts going to execution, engaged in their turn his solicitude and prayers. Cardinals hung about his room, and Popes asked for his miraculous aid in disease, and his ministrations in death. It was his mission to save men, not from, but in, the world. To break the haughtiness of rank, and the fastidiousness of fashion, he gave his penitents public mortifications; to draw the young from the theatres, he opened his Oratory of sacred music; to rescue the careless from the Carnival and its excesses, he set out in pilgrimage to the Seven Basilicas. For those who loved reading, he substituted, for the works of chivalry or the hurtful novels of the day, the true romance and the celestial poetry of the Lives of the Saints. He set one of his disciples to write history against the heretics of that age; another, to treat of the Notes of the Church; a third, to undertake the Martyrs and Christian Antiquities;—for, while in the discourses and devotions of the Oratory, he prescribed the simplicity of the primitive monks, he wished his children, individually and in private, to cultivate all their gifts to the full. He, however, was, after all and in all, their true model, —the humble priest, shrinking from every kind of dignity, or post, or office, and living the greater part of day and night in prayer, in his room or upon the housetop.

And when he died, a continued stream of people, says his biographer, came to see his body, during the two days that it remained in the church, kissing his bier, touching him with their rosaries or their rings, or taking away portions of his hair, or the flowers which were strewed over him; and, among the crowd, persons of every rank and condition were heard lamenting and extolling one who was so lowly, yet so great; who had been so variously endowed, and had been the pupil of so many saintly masters; who had the breadth of view of St. Dominic, the poetry of St. Benedict, the wisdom of St. Ignatius, and all recommended by an unassuming grace and a winning tenderness which were his own.

Would that we, his children of this Oratory, were able, I do not say individually, but even collectively, nor in one generation only, but even in that whole period during which it is destined to continue here, would that we were able to do a work such as his! At least we may take what he was for our pattern, whatever be the standard of our powers and the measure of our success. And certainly it is a consolation that thus much we can say in our own behalf,—that we have gone about his work in the way most likely to gain his blessing upon us, because most like his own. We have not chosen for ourselves any scene of exertion where we might make a noise, but have willingly taken that humble place of service which our Superiors chose for us. The desire of our hearts and our duty went together here. We have deliberately set ourselves down in a populous district, unknown to the great world, and have commenced, as St. Philip did, by ministering chiefly to the poor and lowly. We have gone where we could get no reward from society for our deeds, nor admiration from the acute or learned for our words. We have determined, through God's mercy, not to have the praise or the popularity that the world can give, but, according to our Father's own precept, " to love to be unknown".

May this spirit ever rule us more and more! For me, my dear Fathers of the Oratory, did you ask me, and were I able, to gain some boon for you from St. Philip, which might distinguish you and your successors for the time to come, persecution I would not dare to supplicate for you, as holy men have sometimes supplicated; for the work of the Oratory is a tranquil work, and requires peace and security to do it well. Nor would I ask for you calumny and reproach, for to be slandered is to be talked about, and to some minds notoriety itself is a gratification and a snare. But I would beg for you this privilege, that the public world might never know you for praise or for blame, that you should do a good deal of hard work in your generation, and prosecute many useful labours, and effect a number of religious purposes, and send many souls to heaven, and take men by surprise, how much you were really doing, when they happened to come near enough to see it; but that by the world you should be overlooked, that you should not be known out of your place, that you should work for God alone with a pure heart and single eye, without the distractions of human applause, and should make Him your sole hope, and His eternal heaven your sole aim, and have your reward, not partly here, but fully and entirely hereafter.

Blessed shall you and I be, my dear Fathers, if we learn to live now in the presence of Saints

THE MISSION OF ST. PHILIP. 331

and Angels, who are to be our everlasting companions hereafter. Blessed are we, if we converse habitually with Jesus, Mary, and Joseph, —with the Apostles, Martyrs, and great Fathers of the early Church,—with Sebastian, Laurence, and Cecilia,—with Athanasius, Ambrose, and Augustine,—with Philip, whose children we are, —with our guardian-angels and our patron-saints, careless what men think about us, so that their scorn of us involves no injury to our community, and their misconception of us is no hindrance to their own conversion.

www.ingramcontent.com/pod-product-compliance
Lightning Source LLC
Chambersburg PA
CBHW030326240426
43673CB00040B/1292